PRECEPTS FOR LIVING

PASTOR'S EDITION

UMI

UMI ANNUAL COMMENTARY

PRECEPTS
FOR
LIVING®

PASTOR'S EDITION

MISSION STATEMENT

We are called
of God to create, produce, and distribute
quality Christian education products;
to deliver exemplary customer service;
and to provide quality Christian
educational services, which will empower
God's people, especially within the Black
community, to evangelize, disciple,
and equip people for serving Christ,
His kingdom, and church.

PRECEPTS FOR LIVING® 2020–2021
PASTOR'S EDITION
VOLUME 13
UMI (URBAN MINISTRIES, INC.)

Melvin Banks Sr., LittD, Founder and Chairman
C. Jeffrey Wright, JD, CEO
Cheryl Price, PhD, Vice President of Content

ISBN-13: 978-1-68353-518-8

Publisher: UMI (Urban Ministries, Inc.), Chicago, IL 60643.

To place an order, call us at
1-800-860-8642 or visit us at www.urbanministries.com

Dear Pastor,

Is it your desire to see the people of God increase in their knowledge of His Will, love Him deeply, and follow Him more faithfully? Certainly you'll say "yes" because this is the drumbeat of your heart as a pastor!

It's also why UMI exists. God impressed Hosea 4:6 upon me as a boy in Birmingham, Alabama. The truth of that text resulted in my pioneering the establishment of UMI. Hosea 4:6 (KJV) still rings true today:

"My people are destroyed for lack of knowledge."

This is also why we produce a *Precepts For Living*® Pastor's Edition. We want you to encourage your entire congregation—not just the Sunday School crowd!—to make Bible study a priority during the week. Whether it's at Sunday School, midweek Bible study, another small group gathering, or family devotions, God's people profit from regular exposure to His Word.

Precepts For Living® Pastor's Edition enables you, as pastor, to preach one or more Sunday sermons based on the International Bible Lessons. By doing this, you help strengthen each congregant in his or her understanding and application of God's Word.

We envision this *Precepts For Living*® Pastor's Edition being used along with the *Precepts For Living*® Annual Commentary. The sermons in this volume correlate with the Bible studies in *Precepts For Living*®. That way your sermons can be reinforced by Bible studies in Sunday School or other small groups. In this edition, we anticipate that you will appreciate these sermons presented as outlines and full texts. Additionally, we have included a sampling of sermons for special days. Even if you choose to develop your own sermon from the weekly Bible text, we believe this edition will prove invaluable and will certainly be a catalyst for your preaching.

You will be amazed and delighted at the impact this material will make on your entire congregation. Your church will study a Bible passage and then hear you preach on the same theme or related Bible text.

So enjoy *Precepts For Living*® Pastor's Edition and consider preaching one or more sermons based on the themes or texts. Let us know the result it makes in your congregation.

Sincerely,

Melvin E. Banks Sr, LittD

Melvin E. Banks Sr., LittD

PRECEPTS FOR LIVING®
PASTOR'S EDITION

To maximize your entire congregations' biblical learning experience, this resource will help you correlate some of your sermons with companion Bible studies in the *Precepts For Living®, Annual Commentary*. The continuity between the sermons and the *Precepts* lessons will give further insight into the God-intended meaning of the Scriptures so that your Bible students can successfully understand the principles taught and apply them to their daily living. There are outlines for topical use as well.

LESSON SERMONS

Pastor Rosalyn Bates serves as the Director of Ministries at Southside Worship Center, Chicago, IL. She has a BS in Education & Social Policy from Northwestern University, an MA in Clinical Psychology from Wheaton College, and an MDiv from McCormick Theological Seminary.

Dr. Timothy K. Beougher is the Billy Graham Professor of Evangelism and Church Growth, and associate dean of the Billy Graham School of Missions, Evangelism, and Ministry at Southern Baptist Theological Seminary in Louisville, KY.

Rev. John Burton Jr., MDiv, is a Marketing Communications Consultant and a contributing writer for UMI from Charlotte, NC.

Rev. Jaimie D. Crumley, STM, is a PhD Student at University of California, Los Angeles.

Joshua Edmon serves as an Associate Pastor at Chicago Embassy Church, Chicago, IL.

Pastor Jerome Gay, Jr., is the Lead Pastor at Vision Church, Raleigh, NC.

Pastor Mike Goolsby, a church planter and pastor for the past 14 years, currently functions as the discipleship pastor at a new church plant in Waukegan, IL. Pastor Goolsby holds a degree in Social Science and Communication from Grace College, Winona Lake, IN.

Dr. Daryl R. Hairston, is the Pastor of ACTS Community Baptist Church, Edmond, OK.

Rev. Wayne C. Hopkins, MAT, is a native of Greenville, SC, and pastor of First Timothy Missionary Baptist Church in Los Angeles. He is a graduate of Fuller Theological Seminary and an advocate for bi-vocational pastors across America.

Rev. Matthew C. Jones, DMin, is the Lead Pastor at Del Rey Church, Playa Del Rey, CA.

Rev. Larry Kirk is pastor of Christ Community Church in Daytona Beach, FL.

Rev. Terence K. Leathers, DMin, is the pastor at Mount Vernon Christian Church, Clayton, NC.

Ramon Mayo, MA, is a Senior Innovation Analyst at UMI and the Student Ministry Coordinator for South Suburban Vineyard Church, Flossmoor, IL.

Rev. Joshua Mitchell, DMin, is the Minister of Christian Education and College Students at Wheeler Ave Baptist Church, Houston, TX.

CaReese Mukulu is an analyst and UMI contributor from Chicago, IL.

Pastor Tony Myles, MM, pastors at Riverside Church, Big Lake, MN.

Beth Potterveld, MA, studied Biblical Exegesis at Wheaton College and is now the Developmental Editor for *Precepts for Living* at UMI.

Rev. Cheryl L. Price, PhD, is the Vice President of Content at UMI and an ordained minister, Christian Education workshop developer and presenter, and the author/co-editor of several books and articles.

Pastor Morris Proctor has been a pastor and expository teacher for more than 20 years. He trains preachers through his company, Morris Proctor Seminars, which is based in Murfreesboro, TN.

Pastor Dwight A. Radcliff, Jr., MDiv, is a dedicated husband, father, and the founding pastor of The Message Center World Church in Southern California. He is an Assistant Professor at Fuller Theological Seminary and Director of the Pannell Center for African American Church Studies.

Gina A. S. Robinson, MDiv, STM, is a PhD student at Garrett-Evangelical Theological Seminary.

Allen Reynolds, MDiv, is an Innovation Analyst at UMI. He currently serves as Worship & Adult Education Committee Chair at University Church in Chicago, IL.

Dr. Michael K. Roussell is currently the Presiding Prelate with Chicagoland's Ministerial Alliance, an Ordained Bishop, and an Adjunct Professor with Trinity International University, Deerfield, IL.

Dr. Alvin Sanders is currently the president of World Impact, Inc. Alvin received his MA from Trinity Evangelical Divinity School and a PhD in Educational Leadership from Miami University.

Dr. R. Neal Siler, is the Senior Pastor at First Shiloh Baptist Church, Mechanicsville, VA, and director of The Healing Place Center for Counseling and Spiritual Formation.

Pastor Tommy E. Smith Jr., serves as Senior Pastor at Palma Ceia Baptist Church, Hayward, CA.

Penelope White, MCEd, holds a Community Chaplain's certification and currently serves as a prayer counselor at her church. She previously was the Director of Christian Education for more than two decades.

Rev. Porsha D. Williams, MDiv, is the Pastor to Youth and Children at Bethany Baptist Church, Newark, NJ.

Dr. Melvin Worthington is a pastor and the former executive secretary of the National Association of Free Will Baptists.

Dr. Ricky A. Woods is the senior minister of First Baptist Church West in Charlotte, NC, and a member of the Martin Luther King Chapel Board of Preachers at Morehouse College.

Morgan, Robert. *Nelson's Annual Preacher's Sourcebook*. Nashville, TN. Thomas Nelson, 2001-2006.

Vindicating Eutychus

by Dr. Carolyn Gordon

As a preaching and communication professor, I have heard a plethora of sermons. Some good and others, well… not so good. I am always reluctant to label a sermon absolutely bad, because I know that training, delivery styles, and spiritual gifts vary. In an effort to take inventory of my preaching, I reflected on the worst sermon I ever preached or experienced. It was a sermon I preached one morning at my home church in Kansas City, Missouri. In all honesty, I don't remember the subject matter exactly; I just remember the congregation's blank stares and my subsequent agony of preaching what I considered to be a bad sermon. It felt like the sermon was so awful that people literally wanted to get "unsaved." Yes, I had a vision of congregants lining up before the throne of God requesting that their salvation be revoked. I joked about it to hide the embarrassment, and loved ones assured me that the sermon wasn't quite that bad, but deep down inside, I knew it was bad and that it could never happen again. There is a difference between a sermon badly preached and a bad sermon. The latter is what I hope to never do again.

Another sermon that continues to haunt me is one featured in the documentary *The Most Hated Family in America*. It was a sermon that seemed fueled from some deep dark place within the preacher's soul and accessorized with sarcasm, hatred, and profanity. As I reflected on that sermon, I questioned, "How does one preach a gospel filled with hate in the name of the One who preaches love?" One considers the Apostle Paul's declaration that "it pleased God by the foolishness of preaching to save them that believe." We cannot relegate these types of sermons to mere "foolishness." It is something much more. And it is sometimes that something that keeps us from preaching the Gospel as the Triune God intended. It is that type of sermon that comes from the "dark" dimensions of our souls that can earnestly do damage to the souls of others.

Usually, when a bad sermon is preached, critics point to content, theology, style, or delivery. I contend that the crucial nature of a sermon is not contingent on these factors alone, as evident by the historical record of Jonathan Edwards' sermon "Sinners in the Hands of an Angry God." He reportedly preached from a manuscript, with little vocal variety, facial affect, or gesturing, but that one sermon changed the course of history, helping usher in the First Great Awakening. So what actually constitutes a "bad" sermon? I strongly believe that the physical, emotional, psychological, and spiritual condition of the preacher will dictate more about the quality of their sermon than anything else. In reflection, I realize when I preached my "worst" sermon, I was physically exhausted, emotionally drained, and mentally on a downward spiral. Unbeknownst to me, I was totally burnt out. With self-care, recovery is possible… from both burnout and the bad sermon.

Recently, I heard a preacher referencing Eutychus (Acts 20:7–12) and asserting that if he had been paying attention, he wouldn't have fallen out of the window. He then admonished his hearers, "Don't be like Eutychus… stay awake and quit sleeping through life. If not careful, you might fall out the window just like he did." I have heard this several times and have even preached it on occasion, but this time something was different. Right in the middle of the sermon, I found myself asking, "Why is it that we always blame Eutychus for falling asleep and falling out of that window? Why was it solely his fault and his burden alone? How and when did the lines of demarcation and responsibility get drawn between the pulpit and the pew? And who decided that it's the responsibility of the preacher to preach and the hearers to respond in kind… no matter what?"

In the Scriptures, Paul didn't blame Eutychus for falling asleep and falling out the window. In fact, from his reaction and subsequent response, it appears that Paul felt awful about the situation. Can you imagine someone falling asleep to their own peril, while you are preaching? The Scriptures tell us that Paul had been in the city for about seven days and was planning to leave the next day, so because he had so much to say, he purposed in his heart to preach all night. Can you imagine the kind of physical, mental, and emotional condition Paul must have been in that evening? If nothing else, Paul literally should have been too tired to preach. Yes, the Holy Spirit can empower us to do things that we would not normally be able to do, but we cannot blame the Spirit for our blatant disregard for self-care.

We as clergy have developed a gross disrespect for honoring the Sabbath or rest. We measure our success and value by how busy we are and how much we are in demand. Tired clergy preaching to tired congregations leads to bad sermons, and sometimes to Eutychus falling out of the window. In his book *Say Yes to Grace: How to Burn Bright Without Burning Out*, author and preacher Dr. Kirk Byron Jones argues that many are not operating at their optimum level or creative best because of a lack of sleep and rest. He asserts that without rest, one loses his or her peace, clarity, imagination, creative ability, and a sense of awe for God and humanity. Without these attributes, it is virtually impossible to create a message that would keep Eutychus awake and listening. In fact, clergy must not underestimate the impact that our behavior has on our followers. If we demonstrate resting and honoring the Sabbath, those God has entrusted in our care will know how to do it.

In Genesis, God demonstrated for all of humanity the need to rest. As God has modeled resting for us, we must do the same for others. Modeling rest is a living sermon that can yield miraculous results, including protecting Eutychus from a deadly fall. Thus, the sermon begins long before the preacher mounts the pulpit and utters a single word. In Paul's situation, it is not really about casting fault or blame but figuring out a way to learn now how to keep Eutychus from falling out of the window or the church with effective preaching. For far too long, we have held Eutychus responsible for his own demise. As clergy, I believe that we have a responsibility to preach to those sitting on the outside or the ledges of life. In this case, the reality is a simple one: Eutychus didn't get to the window by himself, and he wouldn't have survived the fall without Paul's assistance.

The world is changing like never before. People now have unlimited access to information and don't always know what to do with this knowledge. Evil is persistently empowered and embraced through racism, sexism, discrimination, abuse, and immorality. Atheism is on the rise. The chasm between the haves and the have-nots is ever-widening. Impatience is rewarded and blind ambition applauded. Many speculate that the next generation will be grossly, apathetically godless and chronically exhausted. Currently, all studies report that church attendance is declining. Perhaps too many people like Eutychus are falling asleep and falling away from Christ while we preach. But, before we can get Eutychus to stay awake in the windows of life, we as clergy must wake up and honestly deal with what is lulling so many hearers to sleep under our watch and what we must do to rectify this phenomenon.

Our callings as preachers, pastors, and ministers are deeply rooted in the commitments we've made to care for the people God has entrusted to us. It is not a call to comfort, popularity, or even constancy—it is a call to reflect the love of God through Christ Jesus. However, in order to care for others, we must take care of ourselves. People are feeling entrapped and enslaved by the pressures, trials, and demands of life. Their cry of hopelessness is deafening. Unfortunately, as preachers, we too are being ravaged by exhaustion and hopelessness. If we are not careful, we can lose our ability to dream new dreams filled with hope and the Gospel, to preach from a place of invigoration and insight. If not careful, one can grow hopelessly stagnant and haphazardly preach from a place of predictability.

As preachers, the challenge for us is to be willing to care for our minds, bodies, and souls. We must be willing to meet challenges with hope and trust in the One who called us and has promised to keep us. It means we must be willing to find new ways to preach the Gospel. It also means we must revisit our Sabbath theology and devise a holy way to rest and care for ourselves. Bad sermons don't always destroy or, in my case, compel hearers to give back their salvation, but bad sermons can cause us to lose Eutychus. Therefore, let's vindicate Eutychus for falling asleep during Paul's sermon by striving to preach better ones to the Eutychuses of today.

Dr. Carolyn Gordon is the Associate Professor of Mass Communication at Mississippi Valley State University. Before relocating to MVSU, she taught at Fuller Theological Seminary and served as Chair of the Preaching and Communication Department.

This essay was edited for length.

Sermon Evaluation Form

At Urban Ministries, Inc., we strive to provide resources that assist in developing and training students, pastors, and preachers to write and deliver sermons that display

- Faithfulness to Scripture
- Concern for the World
- Authenticity from the Messenger
- and Transformative Power

We created this sermon evaluation to serve as a tool for you to assess a given sermon, whether it be yours, a colleague's, or a student's. This tool can be utilized to evaluate either a written or preached sermon.

Ratings: 1 - Outstanding; 2 - Great; 3 - Good; 4 - Satisfactory; 5 - Unsatisfactory

Preacher's Name

Sermon Title

Name of Church

Scripture Passage

Date

---

1. Faithfulness to Scripture

The sermons should be faithful to the words of the text and should provide evidence of close engagement with the main points and issues of it. The sermons should cohere to the larger narrative of God's revelation in Scripture.

Ratings: 1 - Outstanding; 2 - Great; 3 - Good; 4 - Satisfactory; 5 - Unsatisfactory

Section 1

The sermon content demonstrated faithful engagement with Scripture.

1   2   3   4   5

The sermon content helped you understand the Scripture.

1   2   3   4   5

The sermon content illuminated God's presence in the text.

1   2   3   4   5

The sermon content connected the text to God's presence and action in the larger biblical narrative.

1   2   3   4   5

Section 2

Was a main point in the text clearly presented in the sermon? If so, please state your understanding of the main point based on the sermon:

_____

_____

_____

_____

_____

2. Concern for World (Contextual)

The sermon should connect God's presence and activity in the text to the issues in today's world. The sermon should address how the message can be understood in the light of the major social and personal challenges of the listeners.

Ratings: 1 - Outstanding; 2 - Great; 3 - Good; 4 - Satisfactory; 5 - Unsatisfactory

Section 1

The sermon content demonstrated an awareness of today's major issues.

1   2   3   4   5

The sermon content showed a clear connection from the message of the text to a particular problem or issue in the world.

1   2   3   4   5

The sermon content drew appropriate and useful analogies between the biblical world and contemporary society/culture.

1   2   3   4   5

You felt empowered by the sermon to address the concerns in the world or your community.

1   2   3   4   5

Section 2

Please list an example or two of how the sermon resonated with the social context(s) of today's world.

_____

_____

_____

_____

3. Authenticity of the Messenger

The writer or preacher of the sermon should demonstrate that the message in Scripture has convicted him or her at a personal level. Thus, personal engagement and thoughtfulness should be evident in the sermon, with the preacher conveying an authentic voice.

Ratings: 1 - Outstanding; 2 - Great; 3 - Good; 4 - Satisfactory; 5 - Unsatisfactory

Section 1

The preacher approached the text in a genuine way.

1   2   3   4   5

A consistent voice or perspective was presented in an authentic way.

1   2   3   4   5

The preacher conveyed personal engagement and deep thoughtfulness on the text.

1   2   3   4   5

The preacher demonstrated conviction and passion for the topic and text.

1   2   3   4   5

Section 2

Please elaborate on the sense of authenticity you received from the preacher. What confirmed that the messenger was engaged and connected to the text?

_____

_____

_____

_____

4. Transformative Power

The sermons should challenge, encourage, and strengthen your congregation in their attempts to become faithful disciples of Jesus. Message points should use illustrations or scenarios that are relevant and meet listeners' experiences in their daily living. The explication of the text should be easy to apply to any number of situations.

Ratings: 1 - Outstanding; 2 - Great; 3 - Good; 4 - Satisfactory; 5 - Unsatisfactory

Section 1

The sermon content was relevant for challenging, encouraging, and strengthening believers in their journey of Christian discipleship.

1   2   3   4   5

The sermon content lends itself to transformational living for believers.

1   2   3   4   5

The sermons addressed a specific area of life that relates to faithfully living as a believer.

1   2   3   4   5

The sermons contained the potential to be life-changing for a wide range of listeners.

1   2   3   4   5

Section 2

Please comment briefly on the potential for transformative power of the sermon.

_____

_____

_____

_____

_____

_____

5. Sermon Delivery

If applicable, evaluate the preacher on his or her delivery of the given sermon using the following:

Ratings: 1 - Outstanding; 2 - Great; 3 - Good; 4 - Satisfactory; 5 - Unsatisfactory

Section 1

The preacher held a posture and used body language that was fitting for the content of the message.

1   2   3   4   5

The preacher effectively connected to the congregation with consistent eye-contact.

1   2   3   4   5

The preacher delivered the sermon in a clear and understandable tone of voice, and showed variation at appropriate points to place emphasis.

1   2   3   4   5

The preacher showed a deep level of engagement with the message by not simply reading but making it come alive.

1   2   3   4   5

The preacher conveyed a strong sense of confidence in the message and the delivery.

1   2   3   4   5

Section 2

Please comment on the strengths and weaknesses you noticed in the delivery of the sermon.

_____

_____

_____

_____

_____

The Complications of Love

By Dr. Ricky A. Woods

Lesson Theme	Unit Theme	Scripture
Issues of Love	Struggles with Love	Genesis 37:2-11, 23-24, 28

INTRODUCTION

When I was in grade school, the teachers would go to the teacher's lounge after lunch and send the students back to the classroom to take a nap. The teacher would always assign a student to take the names of any student that did not stay in their seat. When the teacher returned to the class, the first item requested was the list of names of possible students that did not obey the rules. Although as students we were all peers, we were also divided by those tattle-tales who had the power to cause the teacher to mete out punishment. No one likes a tattle-tale, no matter how well-intended the teacher may have been. This is similar to the feelings created when Jacob assigned Joseph to watch his brothers in their work and give him a report. Jacob had selected a favorite and doing so changed the family. Whereas it may not be possible to treat all students the same or all children the same, there should be an awareness of possible actions that communicate that some persons matter more than others. Children want to feel valued by the person who leads them, guides them, and prepares them for the future. Love is always complicated because so often we struggle to find the balance to show that all children, and all people for that matter, are valued no matter their birth rank or class rank.

MESSAGE POINTS

Message Point 1: The Problem of Love (Genesis 37:2-4)
Early in Joseph's life, Jacob breaks with the tradition of who would be his heir upon his death and selects not his firstborn son, but Joseph. This selection was due to Joseph's being born to Jacob in his old age. It also likely helped that Joseph is the son of Rachel, the wife that Jacob loved more than Leah. What is clear is that Jacob's selection created family tension.

Joseph's new, elevated status within the family is visualized as a constant reminder to the siblings of his position of favor. Joseph wears a coat of many colors that his father gave him. Joseph is also protected from the hard labor that the other sons of Jacob engaged in, in an agricultural economy. Joseph is made almost a foreman with supervisory responsibility for his older brothers. The effect that Jacob's love for Joseph has on the family is to cause Joseph's brothers to hate him. Whenever expressions of love are restricted to a single individual at the exclusion of others, jealousy, enmity, and danger are near. Such love always creates problems.

Message Point 2: The Pain of Love (vv. 5-11)
There is a saying that goes only a fool tells all that is on their mind. Joseph tells his brothers of a dream that he had, only further revealing his superior status over his brothers. In Joseph's dream, he is not just elevated over his brothers but his brothers are made to bow down to their younger sibling. It is bad enough the brothers had to deal with a tattle-tale now they encounter a story where their subject status to Joseph is intensified. There is

but one interpretation of the dream Joseph tells his brother: it is a dream of rule and dominion in which Joseph is the ruler and his brothers are the subjects that pay homage to him. Joseph's dream reinforces in words what his coat of many colors said visually, that Joseph was special and special meant better. It is not only the words of the dream that anger Joseph's brothers but also the tone in which Joseph shares the dream. Joseph is proud of the dream and the position it puts him in, and Joseph makes sure his brothers know it. So, Joseph's brothers hate him even more. Love can be painful when words injure others intentionally or unintentionally.

Message Point 3: The Plan of Love (vv. 23-24, 28)

When Joseph goes in search of his brothers in the field after sharing his dream with them, Joseph's brothers turn against him. His brothers strip him of his robe of many colors and place Joseph in a pit. The brothers' initial plan is to kill Joseph, but they settle on getting rid of Joseph by selling him to slave traders. The slave traders carry Joseph away to Egypt and sell him again. The once favorite son is now a slave in a foreign land. It would be years before Joseph would see his brothers again. When Joseph sees his brothers, he is no longer a slave, but an official of Egypt. Joseph says to his brothers that God sent him ahead of them to spare their lives from famine. Love – not hate – sent Joseph to Egypt, the love of a God that was with him all the way. Love is complicated. What the love Jacob could not accomplish for Joseph, the love of God did. It was all in the plan of love.

THAT'LL PREACH

Levi Hefner was a courier for Robert E. Lee during the Civil War. Hefner was given a mission to carry a message for General Lee. While carrying the message, Hefner came to a bridge that crossed a creek, and his horse began to balk. Hefner got off the horse to calm him and begins to sing, "Jesus, Lover Of My Soul." When he mounted the horse again to cross the bridge, he kept singing the great hymn. Little did Hefner know that a Union soldier had him in his rifle sight but could not pull the trigger on the man whose hymn reminded the young soldier of his own faith. Years later both men attended a Civil War veteran's reunion and shared their stories of the war. When the Union soldier told of the singing rebel whose life he spared, Hefner cried, "I was that man." That'll preach. Love is complicated, making enemies into allies or brothers into enemies.

CONCLUSION

Love is complicated. Jacob's love for Joseph neglected his older sons and caused them to hate Joseph. God's love for Joseph allows Joseph to be sold into slavery. Yet the day would come when a one-time slave, sold by his brothers, would be the source of deliverance for those same brothers in a famine. Although sometimes complicated, love gives a view of the ways God works to fulfill His purpose for our lives.

NOTES

_____

_____

_____

_____

_____

Promoted

By Dr. Ricky A. Woods

Lesson Theme	Unit Theme	Scripture
God Rewards Obedience	Struggles With Love	Genesis 41:25-33, 37-40, 50-52

INTRODUCTION

Every school year students enter into a new class and grade as a result of being promoted. Students are advanced because they have demonstrated skills, ability, and patience over time to achieve the desired goal. Every year students look forward to being promoted and starting the next phase of their lives. Just as students are promoted, so too are adults when they demonstrated skill and ability in the workplace that adds value to the company. Everyone likes promotions and look forward to being promoted. The day of Joseph's promotion finally came when he was able to interpret Pharaoh's dream. For years Joseph had known the disappointment of being forgotten as he served a sentence for a crime he did not commit. For years Joseph remained faithful in the midst of disappointment, believing that God would reward him in time. Finally, God rewarded Joseph with a promotion that exceeded Joseph's wildest dream. God makes a foreigner second in command of all Egypt. Joseph, the one-time slave, and prisoner rides in the second chariot next to Pharaoh. What a promotion!

MESSAGE POINTS

Message Point 1: Taking Advantage of Opportunity (Genesis 41:25-33)

Joseph's new opportunity is the result of the failure of others. Pharaoh has gone to the men of wisdom in his court but none of them can interpret the dream. No one wants to give Pharaoh bad news. The failure of others to address Pharaoh's concern creates an opportunity for Joseph. The butler who was in prison with Joseph remembered Joseph's ability to interpret dreams and tells Pharaoh about his ability. Sometimes the opportunities that come our way do not reach us by our own merit but are the result of others' failure. To Joseph's credit, when the opportunity comes to use his gifts to change the outcome of a nation as well as his own, he is prepared to seize the moment. We never know just when the opportunity will present itself, and we should always be ready to act and take advantage of the moment. The opportunity before us just might be God's way of preparing the world for the new thing God is about to do. Ask Rosa Parks. We'll get back to her.

Message Point 2: From Prison to the Palace (vv. 37-40)

When Joseph interprets Pharaoh's dream, Pharaoh completely accepts what Joseph has to say as the truth. Pharaoh is willing to hear the bad news about the famine because there is good news about how to prepare for the famine. There is nothing in the interpretation of the dream that threatens Pharaoh's position as a ruler provided that Pharaoh takes the necessary precautions. To Pharaoh's credit, he does not benefit from what Joseph has to say without rewarding Joseph. Pharaoh could have simply commuted Joseph's prison sentence and that would have been reward enough for a man that had spent years in prison. However, Pharaoh does far more; he promotes Joseph and makes him an official of the royal court. Similarly, when God decides to give us a promotion, it is far more than we could have asked or imagined. Joseph is caused to know that God rewards obedience, and he is promoted as a witness to what obedience to God can do.

Message Point 3: Faith and Family (vv. 50-52)

Joseph always had faith while in Egypt, but he had no family. Faith held Joseph to hold on to his values during moments of adversity. Faith allowed Joseph to bear witness to God as a member of Pharaoh's royal court. God responds again to Joseph's faith by providing the one thing that was still missing in his life: a family. Joseph marries a Black woman who loves his pain away. It was the love of a woman that helped Joseph to forget the rejection of his brothers, the lie of Potiphar's wife, being forgotten in prison, and every pain of his past. Joseph's marriage and the children from his marriage help him to start his life anew and know the power of love to heal and to mend. Faith and family bring a level of fulfillment to Joseph's life that he had thought was no longer possible. Joseph's greatest promotion was not being second in command to Pharaoh; his greatest promotion was being a husband and a father.

THAT'LL PREACH

A tired seamstress boarded a Montgomery bus after a long day and just wanted to get home. She took her place on the bus behind the line marked "Colored," but as the bus begins to fill and more whites boarded, the colored section grew smaller and smaller. Finally, the bus driver came and told her she would have to give up her seat. Mrs. Parks refused, not because she was being defiant but because she was tired. Her actions sparked a movement and placed a little-known Georgia preacher, Martin Luther King, Jr., on the national stage. The modern Civil Rights Movement came into being because someone took advantage of the opportunity from the arrest of a tired seamstress who just wanted to go home. I wonder how the bus driver who called the police that night feels about being taken advantage of to start the Civil Rights Movement.

CONCLUSION

Joseph's life changed because God acted on his behalf and gave Joseph a promotion. The promotion did not change who Joseph was. Joseph continued to be a man guided by faith, principles, and values. Joseph's promotion proved that the passage of time does not mean God is unaware of our condition or need. In time God will act to prove His faithfulness to His own. May we remain faithful and obedient in our season of waiting because the promotion God has determined will come!

NOTES

_____

_____

_____

_____

_____

_____

_____

_____

Grace for the victim(izer)?

By Jerome Gay, Jr.

Lesson Theme	Unit Theme	Scripture
Love Versus Guilt	Struggles with Love	Genesis 42:6-25

INTRODUCTION

The idea and concept of justice are universal for all people. However, justice is usually spoken of from one perspective: the victim. Our hearts break for those who have been wronged, especially if harm is done to the defenseless. American history is almost defined by those who have forcibly exercised their power over others. While we cry out for justice to be done on behalf of those who are oppressed, what happens when we are the oppressors? It's easy to plead for mercy when we are the victims, but where are those same cries when we are the victimizers? When we read the history of Joseph and his brothers, we often see things through Joseph's eyes, the victim. But more often than not, we are more like Joseph's brothers, the victimizers. Therefore, it is important to see how they respond to their brother whom they victimized. From their responses, we will learn how we often deny that we're victimizers, how we ought to confess we're victimizers, and how grace is extended to victimizers.

MESSAGE POINTS

Message Point 1: Victimhood mentality breeds victimizers (Genesis 42:6, 9)

Before we discuss how Joseph's brothers responded to him, it's important to highlight what caused them to mistreat their brother. While it makes us uncomfortable to think of ourselves as victims, we sometimes use it to explain why we are in certain situations. It's easy to say, "I'm not allowed to because of 'The Man'" or blame our failures on someone else's success. While these are examples of a victimhood mentality, some truly suffer at the hands of others. Ironically, it's often those who perceive themselves as victims who are the victimizers.

Joseph's brothers hated Joseph for several reasons, but their hate manifested into action when he told them his dream (Genesis 37:5). Joseph dreamed that he would reign and rule over his brothers. Joseph's brothers took offense to this dream and sold him in slavery. Culturally speaking, it is understandable why Joseph's older brothers would take offense at Joseph's dream as those who have been presented with a false narrative of inferiority. However, serving someone younger doesn't mean you are a victim and will somehow be oppressed. Because Joseph's brothers felt like victims, they ended up victimizing their brother. They became the oppressor.

Message Point 2: Response of denial (vv. 7-8)

If we are honest with ourselves, we have all done something similar to Joseph's brothers. We may not have sold our sibling, but we've wronged someone or looked down on someone. And if you can't think of a time, you are likely in denial. Joseph's brothers expressed this same denial. At least fourteen years (Genesis 41:53-54) had passed since Joseph was sold. However, he was still able to recognize his brothers. Sadly, Joseph's brothers were so far removed from their transgression, that they failed to recognize him. Imagine hurting someone and forgetting about it while they carry the scars of your actions.

Not only did they not recognize him, but they also lied and told their father he died (Genesis 37:33). While there was no way for them to know he was alive, they had already concluded Joseph was no more. There seemed to be no remorse or conviction over what they did to their brother. Essentially, they denied anything even happened. How often do we ignore or deny the wrong we've done to someone else?

Message Point 3: Response of conviction (vv. 21-22)

If Joseph had not pressed his brothers, it is likely they would not have acknowledged their guilt. Only when their credibility was tested did they understand justice needed to be served. Generally, when we are faced with the reality of death, we begin to reflect on all the wrong we have done. Our conscience bears witness that we'll have to give an account. Joseph's brothers finally realized that justice is a double-edged sword. They would have to pay for what they did to Joseph.

THAT'LL PREACH

It is undeniable that Joseph exercised his authority quite liberally when it came to his brothers. He had no reason to suspect them of being spies. However, he was trying to teach them a lesson—a lesson so many of us fail to grasp. Grace is only grace because it is given to those who don't deserve it. Joseph had every right to deny his brother's food for what they had done to him. Instead, Joseph gave them food and filled all of their sacks with money. Joseph not only saved his family from starvation but also blessed them with abundance. Is this not what God has done for us? We are not the helpless victims whom Satan terrorizes. Instead, we are his willing accomplices, whom he uses as his instruments to victimize others. We justly deserve God's wrath and judgment, yet it was poured out on the one who can truly claim to be innocent and guilt-free!

CONCLUSION

It is natural to want to extend grace to victims. However, God extends this same grace to victimizers as well. While this may be hard to reconcile, we only need to look in the mirror. How many people have we wronged? Or rather, how many times have you wronged God? It's hard to imagine but God is a victim of our sin. He has done nothing to merit our disobedience, yet we constantly rebel against him. Though God is angered at our sin, He does not respond scornfully, as Joseph's brothers did, but provides salvation and an abundance of blessings. The beauty of the Gospel is God gives grace to the oppressed and He extends grace to the oppressor when they repent!

NOTes

_____

_____

_____

_____

_____

_____

_____

_____

The Puzzling and Perplexing Plan of God!

By Jerome Gay, Jr.

Lesson Theme	Unit Theme	Scripture
God's Plan Revealed	Struggles with Love	Genesis 45:1-15

INTRODUCTION

It is an understatement to say the plans of God surpass all earthly wisdom, not only does His pace surpass our understanding (Philippians 4:7), so does His plan. From our perspective, it is not uncommon to be puzzled and perplexed at God's plan for our lives. We enjoy celebrating the end of someone's journey but fail to appreciate the difficult path it took to get there. What if God gave you a vision that He would put you in a position of authority? However, in order to be placed in this position of authority, your siblings would disown you, you would be accused of rape, and thrown in jail? How many of us would be willing to see this dream become a reality? Though Joseph did not know all the things he would endure, he ultimately understood God had a plan.

MESSAGE POINTS

Message Point 1: God's plan is not thwarted by human decisions (Genesis 45:5)

When Joseph's brothers heard his dream, they thought selling him would prevent it from coming true. Little did they know their decision to exile their brother would lead to their deliverance. From the outside looking in, it would appear their plan was successful. How could their brother rule over them if he was in servitude? Though their decision seemed to thwart God's plan, God worked through their sinful decision to accomplish His plan because His plan can't be stopped.

While Joseph's brothers thought they stopped God's vision for Joseph, we sometimes think we've ruined God's plan for our lives. Although our decisions can have negative consequences, it doesn't mean God now has to resort to a Plan B. God remains in control, even over our decisions, no matter how wrong they may be.

Message Point 2: God's plan may include a famine (vv. 6-7)

Although Joseph benefited during this famine because he was in Egypt, his family didn't. However, God used the famine to teach something to Joseph and his family. The famine taught Joseph that the trials he went through had a purpose: to rescue his family. The famine taught his family that grace is extended despite transgressions.

Far too often, we think God's plan doesn't involve suffering. However, it's possible that God's plan for our lives primarily includes suffering (2 Timothy 2:12). It's usually during times of spiritual "famine" when we recognize we are completely hopeless and throw ourselves at God's mercy. Therefore, God uses times of famine to strengthen our faith.

Message Point 3: Acknowledge the providence of God's plan (v. 8)

Despite Joseph's tumultuous journey, he constantly acknowledged God's providence. He didn't hold his brothers in contempt but understood God sent him. He understood God allowed the famine so that he could save his family. He also understood it was ultimately God, not Pharaoh who made him ruler over all the land of Egypt.

Joseph made sure he acknowledged God for being in this position of authority. However, we generally acknowledge God only when things work in our favor. Joseph could have easily held a grudge against his brothers, but he understood God allowed it all to happen for a reason. This does not absolve one of wrongdoing, but it leaves justice and retribution to God.

THAT'LL PREACH

 Understanding how God works is such a paradox. It seems backward that God would use the hatred and jealousy of Joseph's brothers to lead to their salvation. However, God consistently confounds human wisdom. This reality is chiefly seen in the Gospel. At Pentecost, Peter says one of the most puzzling things in all of Scripture. He says, "[Jesus,] being delivered by the determinate counsel and foreknowledge of God, ye have taken, and by wicked hands have crucified and slain" (Acts 2:23). Why would God's plan of salvation include having His only begotten Son killed in one of the most gruesome ways ever? Not only that but He still holds those accountable for killing Jesus, even though it ultimately led to salvation. Essentially, we cannot comprehend the mind and plans of God. We simply need to trust that God will get great glory for Himself and that we are privileged to benefit from His puzzling and perplexing plans.

CONCLUSION

Unfortunately, trusting that God has a plan is easier said than done because God's plan often includes suffering. Joseph and his family suffered. However, their suffering leads to their redemption. While this is a great story of redemption, they did not know how it would end. Neither Joseph nor his family knew redemption would follow after suffering. Admittedly, we don't know what we'll encounter in life, but we do know how God's plan ends. We may be puzzled and perplexed at God's plan for our lives, however, we should find comfort knowing He has a plan. We don't know what the future holds, but we can take comfort in knowing who holds our future (Psalm 16:5).

NOTES

_____

_____

_____

_____

_____

_____

_____

_____

Lean On Me

By Tony Myles

Lesson Theme	Unit Theme	Scripture
Love and Devotion to Others	What Is Love?	1 Samuel 19:1-7

INTRODUCTION

Ever notice the horrible math often used in so many friendships? We might listen only half of the time. We tend to discern only a quarter of what we hear. We could think zero about what our friends are thinking about 100% of the time. We can choose to double-down on anything offensive.

And yet all of these numbers have something in common—they all begin with one. Every friendship or family connection is shaped by the actions of many but can be reshaped by the actions of one. The love and devotion that we choose to embrace or reject affect everyone else around us. We see this especially played out in the lives of David, Jonathan, Saul, the immediate family, and the entire Israelite kingdom as each person chose a role that shaped all the others.

MESSAGE POINTS

Message Point 1: Friends are responsive in light of rejection (1 Samuel 19:1-3)

First Samuel 18 details Saul's insecure fear of David, primarily due to David's growing public favor among the masses and new personal relationships with Saul's family. There was also a matter of an evil spirit that tormented Saul (1 Samuel 18:10), which prompted the first violent attack against David. All of that spilled over into this defining moment when Jonathan, Saul's son, had to choose between blind support of his father in all his violence or a godly allegiance to David. Jonathan hadn't yet made up his mind, though. What was clear was that his friend was experiencing rejection and he could be responsive about it in some way.

Message Point 2: Family is inquisitive in light of confusion (vv. 4-5)

If this chapter provided all we knew about Jonathan, we could credibly summarize that he was a man of honor. His new friendship with David mattered, but so did his historical family relationship with his father. It was out of this integrity that he attempted to guide Saul into a better frame of mind by out-truthing the feelings of insecurity that the king was living out of. It was a powerful, transformational union of love and leadership that essentially asked, "Dad, help me understand why you would even think to do this when David has clearly been for you and not against you." When a family member is confused, we help them with questions. But questions are only at their best when they aren't antagonistic but helps others recognize that we wrestle not against flesh and blood but against the evil in this world (Ephesians 6:12) trying to make its way into us.

Message Point 3: Devotion is loyal in light of choice (vv. 6-7)

In one moment, everything can be changed. Through Jonathan's help, Saul had a renewed moment of sanity about David that allowed him to choose devotion among all the possible choices before him. Within the great

9

scope of free will and the tremendous gift it is, though, there is a shadow to it all in that devotion must continue to be chosen daily. As time went on, Saul lapsed in this and went on to set himself against David more dramatically. This calls us to recognize that a friendly agreement is not the same as a humbled resolution, for the former is all about getting rid of the bad circumstances while the latter is all about the investment of love beyond the negative situation. Only by a healthy feeding of care can that which was starved become vibrant and stronger than it was before.

THAT'LL PREACH

Likely, we've all made a mistake while dressing ourselves in the dark, be it putting on a shirt backward with the tags sticking out or selecting two socks that looked the same in the shadows but were actually quite different (as you discovered later in the day to some embarrassment). This is the reality that 1 Corinthians 13:12 speaks of, in that life right now is like seeing through a dark glass, which means we only know things "in part." This all permanently changes in eternity when things are made fully known, but for the time being, we have to constantly remind ourselves that every situation or relationship in our lives is dimly lit. Only by placing ourselves near the light of God through His Bible, church, and presence can we better gauge if how we're treating others has been tagged correctly or if we've read things wrong and it's time to put a sock in it.

CONCLUSION

It's great that Saul listened to Jonathan and decided not to hurt David. However, this doesn't mean that Saul used Jonathan's words as a way to listen to God. Only the Lord can create lasting transformation, which means true love and loyalty has to come out of our relationship with Him. It's a very thin-yet-very-thick line that Jonathan evidenced but his dad did not. Let's not be the kind of people who just try to do good or the right thing, but instead, be people who are becoming good out of our right relationship with Jesus.

NOTES

_____

_____

_____

_____

_____

_____

_____

_____

The Solution to Moldy Relationships

By Tony Myles

Lesson Theme	Unit Theme	Scripture
Love Your Enemies	What Is Love?	Luke 6:27-36

INTRODUCTION

Black mold is toxic and nobody's friend, be it homeowner, resident, or guest. This quite dangerous growth begins in areas of a home that are uniquely humid or damp, such as basements and crawlspaces. Anyone who spends any length of time around it (even if not immediately seeing it) can experience a range of allergies or health issues that include chronic fatigue, headaches, fevers, rashes, and irritations all over. Some extreme cases can lead to vomiting and internal bleeding, all before it even emerges and is visible for what it's been allowed to grow into.

The analogy couldn't be clearer when it comes to what we let grow in antagonistic relationships. The "black mold" between us and another person can't be wiped away with one dry swipe but requires meticulous care and cleaning to make sure we haven't missed something toxic. Jesus says that love toward those we deem our enemies is the only solution that can truly penetrate.

MESSAGE POINTS

Message Point 1: Listening leads to loving (Luke 6:27-28)

It's absurd to think of, but even Jesus as a Master Teacher had to rally His listeners to pay attention in class. The Israelites heard the 101 version centuries earlier through Moses, but now Jesus was teaching the 401 level of instruction. This is why, before His list of what to do and what not to do, He essentially said, "If you're willing to listen to Me, it'll change how you understand what I ask you to do." God knows it's easier to grow weary in doing good when we're just trying to do good, but personally listening to Him means personally noticing Him. This type of listening also better equips us to personalize how we see other people, opening up the door for us to let love for the person overtake any frustration over a circumstance.

Message Point 2: Loving leads to stretching (vv. 29-34)

One of the things Jesus continually asks throughout His ministry was that His followers would see through the broken systems of the day and instead reveal His Kingdom on earth as it is in heaven. At times He had to correct even His closest followers by warning them that what they did (even with the best of intentions) didn't serve Him or the greater thing He was doing. We could observe a modern-day version of this in how we commonly let there be space between us and another person for unhealthy periods instead of proactively working on things. Jesus calls us not to build walls but bridges, so we don't get so used to the way things are that we neglect claiming what they could actually become. Loving always leads to stretching—the kind that shows we're all in, even when someone is pulling out. Only by reaching out can we close the gap and better see each other face to face.

Message Point 3: Stretching leads to receiving (vv. 35-36)

The Scriptures are filled with wisdom on how living for God can turn enemies into friends. Proverbs 16:7 speaks directly to this, and Matthew 18:19 says that when two or three people come together, even in the midst of sin, Jesus' presence is revealed. This can be true even in the sharpest of divisions, be it among those who don't like you politically, professionally, socially, or otherwise. Blessing our enemies helps them see us as a blessing, which in turn opens them up to receive us and Christ in us. While the broken system of frustration leading the way may be common, Christians must seek the truer system of reconciliation. We can choose to not let blood be spilled between us and another person because Jesus already spilled His blood for us at the Cross.

THAT'LL PREACH

Sometimes in our attempt to claim a victory with another person, we overlook how we already have it through God. Consider how during an epic conflict of war (2 Chronicles 20), King Jehoshaphat sought God through prayer and fasting about how to face his enemies. He resolved to send worship singers ahead of his army who would proclaim God's identity and the people's allegiance. Imagine being one of those singers on the front line and heading into harm's way, while knowing that every praise on your lips claimed God's faithfulness and enduring love.

Personalize that by imagining your version of this in whatever unique tensions or battles you're facing. You may not be able to control the war, but you can go into confusing battles with a clear relationship before God. What would it look like to claim His presence over your past, present, and future (including the situation you're in)? How will you let your worship of an everlasting Lord inform what's possible in the timely thing before you?

CONCLUSION

Our culture has created multiple "weapons of war" that have adapted over time: First, we used our fist. Then, a rock. Soon we developed the club, mace, sword, and arrow. Eventually, we created bombs, bullets, missiles, chemical warfare, and technological terrorism. Meanwhile, Jesus' weapon of choice hasn't changed, He calls us to use the love that He first pours into our hearts so it can overflow into the heart of our relationships.

NOTES

_____

_____

_____

_____

_____

_____

_____

_____

_____

Strange Neighbors

By Dr. Alvin Sanders

Lesson Theme	Unit Theme	Scripture
Loving Your Neighbor	What Is Love?	Luke 10:25-37

INTRODUCTION

The average Christian has been exposed to what a colleague of mine referred to as "Reconciliation 101," meaning they had an introduction to the topic at some point in their life. Before 1950, the cultural norm was segregation. The concepts of integration and equal rights really began to take root in the 1960s. With legal victories, a new paradigm began to take shape: multiculturalism.

Before the '70s, the spotlight had been on assimilation into an American "melting pot." But then multiculturalism began to take root. Multiculturalism might be thought of as a "salad." It is considered one meal; however, the tomato remains a tomato, lettuce remains lettuce, and croutons remain croutons. Like a salad, in multiculturalism, each culture keeps its distinctive characteristics. While it is possible to celebrate these distinctions, they can also cause division.

Multiculturalism has evolved into cultural diversity. Corporate America discovered that it was good business to address and market based on race, ethnicity, gender, and other cultural categories. Cultural diversity goes beyond just the acknowledgment of different cultures. If we use the metaphor of a salad for multiculturalism, cultural diversity is a salad that tastes good. It is the intentional working toward being culturally competent.

I think our racial division is a symptom of a much larger issue of Christians not understanding the role of culture in their lives. Christians need to embrace a fundamentally different way of responding to cultural differences, grounded in the biblical story of the Good Samaritan, showing reconciliation as the mission of God in our fallen world.

MESSAGE POINTS

Message Point 1: Radical Transformation (Luke 10:25–37)

A Jewish Law expert asks Jesus what he must do to inherit eternal life. Jesus answers with a question, asking what is written in the Law. The expert, in turn, answers by quoting Deuteronomy 6:5 and Leviticus 19:18: to love God with all your heart, soul, and mind and love your neighbor as yourself. Digging into the Leviticus law, the expert asks Jesus, "Who is my neighbor?" (v. 29). Jesus answers by sharing the parable of the Good Samaritan. Jesus, by telling that story, was emphasizing that loving God should cause a radical transformation of how you treat people, especially those who are different from you. We see in this story not only reconciliation along ethnic lines but also across economic ones, as the one who has plenty takes care of the one who does not have enough. We also see reconciliation across power lines, as the marginalized (Samaritan) show compassion to the powerful (the Jew).

Message Point 2: Loving the Stranger (vv. 33–34)

In other words, Jesus says loving God includes loving the cultural stranger. Many people buy into the responsibility to love those who are culturally like themselves. What about the cultural stranger? The Jewish people have long been told to welcome them (Leviticus 19:34). But also have a history of mistrusting outsiders who might pollute their religion. Jesus says we are nearest to eternal life, however, when we love the stranger too. In fact, He tells the story so that the role model for us to follow showing us what loving our neighbor means—is himself a foreigner.

Message Point 3: Connecting Belief to Action (vv. 36–37)

In verses 36 and 37, we see Jesus end His teaching by asking a question to make sure that the expert understood His corrective teaching of the expert's limited cultural definition of a neighbor. The expert's reply ("He that shewed mercy") shows that he did (v. 37). Jesus then commands the expert to apply his right belief with the right action ("Go, and do thou likewise," v. 37). In order to be reconcilers, we must act on our Christian beliefs and turn them into powerful actions.

THAT'LL PREACH

One of my favorite TV shows is *Flip This House*. This program follows the lives of real estate developers in many cities. They buy homes, renovate them, and resell them for a profit. The challenge is to look at your life as a brick house. Each one of the bricks represents an experience. Some experiences are good, and some are awful. Nevertheless, they are your bricks. When Jesus comes in, He is the real estate developer, creating something brand new (2 Corinthians 5:17). He is rehabbing you for your profit.

CONCLUSION

When it comes to reconciliation, some of us have had the gift of having many good bricks used during our original construction. We have had positive life experiences through marrying a person of another race or ethnicity, or having great friendships with people in poverty, or having wonderful women in our lives. Those of us with an overabundance of these types of experiences embrace reconciliation very easily. However, most people need to be rehabbed. They have experiences of being mistreated because of their social class, practicing discrimination against other ethnicities, or growing up thinking that women don't have the same gifting and abilities to contribute at the same level of men in God's kingdom. The bad news is that these types of bricks don't just go away. The Good News of the Gospel is that if you so desire you can be rehabbed by God. You can also share with others this rehab process. In fact, the story of Luke 10:25–37 says that if your faith is to be authentic, you really have no choice in the matter. You were told to go and do likewise. So let the house flip begin!

NOTES

_____

_____

_____

_____

_____

Lasting Love

By Melvin Worthingtom

Lesson Theme	Unit Theme	Scripture
Love Divine	What is Love?	1 Corinthians 13

INTRODUCTION

According to the *Knoxville News Sentinel*, Police Chief Phil Keith was in the middle of a city council meeting in Knoxville, Tennessee, when his pager beeped. Startled to see that the call was from his mother, he rushed to the press table and phoned her. "Phil Keith, are you chewing gum?" demanded his mom, who had been watching on TV. "Yes, ma'am."

"Well, it looks awful. Spit it out." Keith dutifully removed the gum and went back to his meeting. There's no one like mothers! The words "mother" and "love" go together like left and right hands, and on this Sunday, there's no better passage to study than the "Love Chapter" of the Bible which describes the agape love of God which is necessary for mothers, fathers, sons, daughters, and all the rest of us.

MESSAGE POINTS

Message Point 1: The Place of Love (1 Corinthians 13:1-3)

Love is superior to eloquent words (v. 1). Love is the vital principle, and without it, all other endowments, including excellence in communication, are in vain. Love is superior to wisdom (v. 2). If a person could unlock the mysteries of the entire universe and call forth faith to remove mountains, he would be zero without love. Love is superior to work (v. 3). More important than saying the right thing, knowing the right thing, or even going through the right motions, is to do it all in love.

Message Point 2: The Portrait of Love (vv. 4-7)

Love is patient (v. 4). It bears injustice without anger or despair. Love may be practiced (v. 4). It is mild under all provocations and ill-usage. Love produces good manners and courtesy at all times. Love is pure (v. 4), not jealous or displeased when others are successful. Love never embarrasses the owner or recipient. Love is peaceful (v. 4). It is not rash. Love takes a back seat and is willing to work behind the scenes. Love does not brag or boast or sing its own praises. Love is polite (v. 5), doing nothing to cause shame. Love prefers others (v. 5). There is no selfishness in true love. It seeks the good of others. Love is not easily provoked (v. 5). When love holds the reins of the soul, there is little danger of provocation to anger and spiteful action that leads to sin. Love is inclusive (v. 5). It does not condemn on suspicion or without evidence, nor is it malicious nor disposed to find fault. Love exhibits propriety (v. 6). It does not sympathize with evil, nor does it delight in anything that does not conform to the standard of right. Love takes pleasure in truth (v. 6). Love rejoices in the virtues of others, not their vices. Love is pleasant (v. 7). Love maintains a disposition that refuses to make public or to avenge the faults of others. Love is not suspicious. It trusts others. Love brightens all things, bears all things and braves all things.

Message Point 3: The Permanence of Love (vv. 8-13)

Love's permanency is suggested by the phrase "love never fails" (v. 8). Love will always abide, may always be exercised, and can be adapted to all circumstances in which we may be placed. Love's pre-eminence is suggested by the phrase "but the greatest of these is love" (v. 13). Love is the greatest of all gifts, for love makes the rest of the gifts graceful. Love is the one needful thing—our priority. We can lose our goods or even our good names, but if we truly retain love, we have exchanged the temporary for the eternal. The Bible has said all it will say about God, contained in the one statement: "God is love" (1 John 4:8).

THAT'LL PREACH

F. E. Marsh tells of some young pastors who paid a visit to one of the great ministers of the past generation. They found him preparing to go to a meeting where a strong debate was expected. He was reading the 13th chapter of 1 Corinthians and praying that its teaching might guide his conduct. The aged minister felt the need for the restraining hand of divine grace and the calming power of love, lest he should be rash in his speech. This is the kind of love that lasts.

CONCLUSION

Maybe the mother in your life already shows all these loving characteristics. Even if she does—or I should say *because* she does, I bet she still studies them as thoroughly as Mr. Marsh did. It's a lot to live up to. As we have seen, though love is better than any other gifting of the Spirit, more lasting, and more needed. May the love of God guide us all.

NOTES

_____

_____

_____

_____

_____

_____

_____

_____

_____

_____

_____

Passing the Love Test

By Wayne C. Hopkins

Lesson Theme	Unit Theme	Scripture
Loving By Serving	Godly Love Among Believers	John 13:1-15, 34-35

INTRODUCTION

James and Ruby married at age 18. Unlike their peers, they genuinely loved each other and saved their sexual purity for marriage. Being so young, they had a full set of living parents, grandparents, and even great-grandparents who soon became impatient at the young couple remaining childless. Still not parents by 28, family and friends began to question what they were doing wrong. Suggestions swirled, presuming some moral failure was at work. Privately, James and Ruby knew that a child would be a gift from God and after their eleventh anniversary, their daughter was born. James and Ruby were no longer the young teens they had once been. Their relationship was strained by working little princess Jasmine into their schedules. One night James struggled to keep the baby quiet while Ruby slept. He felt like a failure as the baby cried and his body ached. Just as he changed yet another diaper, Jasmine began to smile and giggle, making her daddy burst with joy over nothing more than seeing his little angel happy. In that quick moment, James had changed this baby's life from misery to unspeakable joy. James hated diaper duty, but he loved his child with all his heart!

MESSAGE POINTS

Message Point 1: Love is Thorough (John 13:1-2)

The text is rich with imagery that connects Christ to the Old Testament. The original Passover required the sacrifice of a lamb and spreading its blood on the doorposts, thereby protecting the Children of Israel from the death angel (Exodus 12:3-13). Now, Christ is in the beginning stages of His own passion, as He prepares to shed His own blood on the Cross. John 13:1 says Jesus loved them "to the end." This is no surprise, as He had chosen them, appointed and instructed them, and had led them in a unique relationship, unlike anything we have seen since. Jesus personally trained His disciples for the work of preaching the Gospel. He did not choose them for their eloquence or their pedigree. He chose them as examples of the diversity of humanity, all of which would need a Savior.

Message Point 2: Love is Tested: (vv. 2, 5-8)

Jesus' demonstration of love is very much a term of action—a viable verb in every sense. The Greek word 'agapao' describes love as 'being pleased by' something or someone. We are encouraged throughout Scripture to desire to please God, yet, God's love is unique in that we cannot discern *why* or *how* He finds pleasure in us—He simply does. Even with unconditional love hard at work, it is clear that its limits are tested. Jesus is aware that He will be betrayed. He knows precisely who will commit the crime. Yet, He continues to love the disciples, the faithful and the failed. He serves them a final Passover meal, then He proceeds to wash their feet—yet another act of selfless love. Even without a deep understanding of ancient Jewish culture, we all know the extreme conditions under which we will even look at each other's feet, let alone wash them! This surely tests the limits of our love, but it is literally nothing for Jesus. His commitment to demonstrating service, rather than simply controlling behavior, proves that Jesus' love is not only abundant, it is strong enough to withstand any test.

Message Point 3: Love is Triumphant (vv. 8-10, 34-35)

Peter and Judas were not the only ones putting Jesus' love to the test. All the disciples' lack of obedience and understanding only underscored the true nature of God's love. We can never earn it or deserve it. All we can do is be thankful for it. Peter's valiant attempt to preserve Jesus' dignity by at first refusing to have his feet washed demonstrates that we embrace sin easier than we accept God's offer of love. Once Jesus explained his motivations, Peter immediately flips in favor of a double portion. Judas and the other disciples' silence represents the range of apathy, atrophy, and agony evident in the world. Some feel entitled, others feel drained, and some have no concept at all that they are the objects of God's love. This is how we know the Gospel message is as necessary as it is true. Christ's "new commandment" firmly establishes love as triumphant over all things in this world. It is the eradicator of sin, it is the healer of souls, and it binds us together with each other, as with the Lord. Love Wins!

THAT'LL PREACH

A young lady was once injured in a catastrophic car accident. Although she had been engaged to be married, the wedding had to be postponed due to her extended time of recovery. While she remained in good spirits, she realized her body would not ever return to its former state. Despite her family's encouragement, she resigned herself to placing marriage on hold indefinitely so she could simply focus on learning her new way of life. The only problem was her fiancé had no plans of letting her enter any new life without him! They argued until she told him he was no longer welcome in her hospital room. She told him to go on with his life. The next morning, the young lady woke to her mom fixing her hair. Soon her sisters came and began putting flowers all over the room. Finally, her fiancé came in, followed by the rest of their families and the hospital chaplain. Before the young lady could protest, her fiancé knelt by her bed and through tears began to recite his vows and pledge on the spot.

CONCLUSION

Romans 8 dares us to find something more powerful than God's love. We separate ourselves through sin, yet God through Christ is adamant that our sinful state is not to be our final destination. Jesus said, "I and my Father are one" (John 10:30). The love of God is manifested through Christ's sacrifice and we receive and understand it only by the power of the Holy Spirit. Whether we believe it or not, to be alive is to be loved. The least we can do is follow Jesus' example and show that love to one another in every possible way.

NOTES

_____

_____

_____

_____

_____

_____

How Is Your Love Life?

By Wayne C. Hopkins

Lesson Theme		Unit Theme		Scripture
Abiding Love		Godly Love Among Believers		John 15:4-17

INTRODUCTION

Our society is obsessed with the alleged love affairs of celebrities and athletes. People snoop for every shred of information about who's hooking up and who's cheating, then they will turn around and celebrate a second third or fourth marriage of someone only previously busted for a scandalous situation. What if we were to redirect the camera's lens from minding others' business and begin taking a paparazzi-style look at our own lives? Is it evident that we love God? Do we acknowledge and celebrate God's love in our lives? It's time to look at the kind of love God has for us and make sure we are in the right relationship!

MESSAGE POINTS

Message Point 1: Love Is Not An Accessory, It's A Necessity (John 15:4-5)

Jesus presents Himself in a beautiful analogy featuring a vine, its branches, and the fruit they eventually bear. He understands human nature causes us to pull away and attempt to separate from God, yet we are totally dependent upon God. He says we cannot bear fruit if we are disconnected; and in verse 5 He says without God or separate from God, we can do absolutely nothing. An agnostic may claim not to know what to believe about God, and an atheist will declare there is no God at all, but what if God declared an end to humanity? We are far too caught up in our desire to choose our own path. It is God who extends His life-giving love to us throughout every day, every moment, every breath. We can certainly try to live without it, but there is nothing optional about God.

Message Point 2: Love is Filling to the Empty Soul (vv. 7-11)

Most love in human interaction ends up one-sided. We love our pets, but they don't feed us or provide for our medical care—all they do is bark, purr, or otherwise be a creature of comfort. Even in more romantic or friendship situations, one of us usually leans on the other without much of a result beyond comfort and companionship. God, however, makes it clear that when we are connected with His true vine, we are engaged with a source of energy, provision, sustenance, and ultimately joy that can't be described. Romans 5:8 says that God commends His love to us so that even as sinners, we have access to a Savior who will clean us, change us, restore us, and fill us with His unspeakable joy. While Fido and Fifi, Frank, and Felicia can make us feel better for a moment, God desires for us to be in a better place for eternity. That is a sign of true love.

Message Point 3: The More Love We Get, The More Love We Give (vv. 12-17)

Why does Jesus emphasize love as a commandment? Should not such an intimate and emotional expression be done purely of free will and desire? Technically, it is, but not ours. Our free will and desire can change the moment the weather shifts or our stomach groans in hunger. We express the deepest most passionate love while watching our favorite teams play, then switch to the most heinous hatred the moment someone fumbles the ball. In life, we are fine with people who enable our quirks, overlook our attitudes, and generally avoid holding us accountable. Yet the moment someone speaks the truth in our face, we are ready to fight. Jesus commands love because it should be mindful. It should be purposeful. It should be an effort that is made, a choice that is set forth—an objective and a mission so that we are carrying the love of Christ with us. We fear that our joy cannot be full if another person is as well. But in truth, the more love we share, the more we receive. God has loved us beyond our failures and accomplishments. He's loved us in spite of what we have done and what we may become. God's vision of our love life is one where our friendships become family, our marriages produce legacies, and our hearts reach out to those in need.

THAT'LL PREACH

Two families held a powerful influence in a small church. They both had elders, young adults, and youth who seemed to stay close enough to remain in the congregation, but at opposite ends of unity. New members were recruited not to ministries, but to choose sides, seeing as there was no middle ground. While everyone claimed to be loving in public, the truth was just under the surface. During one particularly heated church meeting, one of the grandmothers in one of the families launched an attack on the deacon from the other family. In the midst of their shouting, she gasped for air and collapsed into the deacon's arms. Having barely a civil word for 30 plus years, everyone froze in place. The deacon, however, was trained in CPR and tended to the matter at hand. Every day for the next week, he sat at her hospital bedside, defying unspoken family codes and mystifying family friends and congregation. On the day grandmother was lucid again, the first face she saw was the person she had attacked as an enemy. He simply said, "You won the fight!"

CONCLUSION

Love has been made mysterious by a world consumed with power and lust. The truth of the matter, however, is that God is love (1 John 4:16). If we have any connection with God at all, we know we are loved, and we have been given a portion of love to share with others. The more we give, the more we will get, and that's good!

NOTES

_____

_____

_____

_____

_____

_____

_____

_____

There is Love in the Soup

By Dr. Terence K. Leathers

Lesson Theme	Unit Theme	Scripture
Confident Love	Godly Love Among Believers	1 John 3:11–24

INTRODUCTION

In 2015, while on a summer vacation with my wife and daughter, I happened to turn on the news and hear what was to be an astonishing story. The news anchor reported that on June 19, of that year, only two days after a racist white gunman shot and killed nine people during Bible study in a Black church in Charleston, South Carolina, relatives of the victims offered him forgiveness. At first, it seemed unbelievable to me that the word "forgiveness" could come from the family member's mouth with such ease, especially as I saw the redness in her eyes and the worry on her face. But then I remembered what I had heard before—"If you don't forgive, it eats you up from the inside out." One writer has stated that "to forgive is necessary food for the soul." For me, love will eventually wear down the chain of hate thereby chaining the status quo.

MESSAGE POINTS

Message Point 1: The Main Ingredient (1 John 3:11-12)

John makes it crystal clear in this Scripture that one ingredient rules the day. He gives an indication, as taught by Master Chef Jesus, that we have an intense and holy responsibility to love one another. Humanity's soup is lacking in taste, flavor, and quality for our existence if the ingredient is known as "love" is left out. We may be able to deviate from other recipes and add a substitute ingredient that might be sufficient in satisfying our taste. But there is no substitute for God's love. Gospel singer and songwriter VaShawn Mitchell sums it all up in his gospel song, "Nobody Greater." He says, "[I] searched all over couldn't find nobody, I looked high and low still couldn't find nobody. Nobody greater, nobody greater no, no nobody greater than you." There is nobody greater than God because He provides the ingredient known as love to a world lost in sin.

Message Point 2: A Fly in the Soup (vv. 13-18)

Although we are given the responsibility to love one another, John indicates that if we want humanity's soup to have love as its base ingredient, we must avoid adding the seasonings known as evil and hate. In fact, we ought to remove them from our spiritual seasoning rack. Cain had introduced these ingredients into humanity's soup by killing his brother Abel. As a result of his action, we could have become compromised people. We could have accepted standards that were lower than what God desired for us. But because of the righteousness of Abel in spite of his death, we can have an abiding link with Jesus because God's love and righteousness abide in Him. Passing from death to eternal life is a Christian norm. This means that a change has come over you. Our old selves, our old ways of doing things are discarded or abandoned so that Jesus can link His righteousness to the path we must follow as a peculiar people.

Message Point 3: Soup's On (vv. 19-24)

The death of Abel called for humanity's table to be set and the sanctified soup to be served. Now there was a need for the main course. The main course—known as Jesus—had laid His life down for us so that we could experience, taste, see, and feel a perfect and saving love. There is no need for our hearts to be broken or condemned by what we have done. Just as Jesus showed His love for us, we (those of us who know Him) have an unspoken mandate to give of ourselves to help somebody who may be in need. If we can follow Master Chef Jesus and open our hearts up such that our service to others flows freely and uninhibited, we can make a difference in the lives of so many who may have lost their way and strayed from the dinner table of God's amazing love. If we can keep His commandments and abide in Him, His spirit will give us the strength to love everybody even those who may wound our spirit and seek to trouble our lives.

THAT'LL PREACH

 I have often pondered the statement, "Love don't cost a thing," especially as it relates to loving those who have broken your heart, mistreated you, caused trouble in your life or the life of someone you love. The truth is love can cost you worry concerning the trial of someone who may have injured your beloved family member. It can cost you anxiety, loss of sleep, the development of bad habits, and self-esteem issues because someone may have been taken away from you violently or unexpectedly. But what's comforting for me is to know that Jesus has a unique sensibility to our needs and status regarding our existence. As such, those of us who have had some encounters with Jesus know that He negates the cost because, on Cavalry's hill, He paid it all. The account has been closed, and the debt has been paid.

CONCLUSION

As we press this word close to our hearts, let us remember that love rules the day. Whatever we do, let us not season our love meal with the seasonings of evil and hate. In fact, if and when you can, banish those seasonings from the seasoning rack known as your heart. Then sit down and graciously thank God for the main course. If you will, thank God for sending Jesus and allowing Him to give His life so that we might have life and live more abundantly.

NOTES

_____

_____

_____

_____

_____

_____

_____

_____

All I have is HIS

By Dr. Terence K. Leathers

Lesson Theme	Unit Theme	Scripture
Sharing Love	Godly Love Among Believers	Acts 4:32-5:11

INTRODUCTION

Early in my youth, one of the songs that greatly impacted and influenced my life and certainly my development as a Christian was "I Surrender All." In accompanying my father to church revivals and homecomings whether in rural areas or cities, someone (usually a senior church mother) would sing that song. This song carried an air of significance in the hearts and minds of all who sat, stood or found themselves in the building or under the revival tent. I believe that this song had such a profound impact on me because it suggested that everything I had belonged to Jesus and that my attitude should be one of acknowledgment and acceptance of that fact. I believed that this song echoed my obedience to and recognition of a God worthy to be served.

MESSAGE POINTS

Message Point 1: Harmony in the Hood (Acts 4:32-35)

The beginning of this text indicates that the believers in Jesus were of one heart and soul. They shared their possessions and they worked together for the good of their fellow believers. They exhibited a sense of responsibility for the other, and all of what they did was centered on Jesus and God's Grace. For me and those of my generation, this kind of "harmony in the hood" was perhaps best represented on TV in *The Andy Griffith Show*. The show represented a time when people knew their neighbors by their first name. They had everything in common. They hung out at one another's homes, worshiped together, and even provided Otis, the town drunk, a place to lay his head when he couldn't make it home. There was "harmony in the hood," and there was "the peace of God which surpasses all understanding" (Philippians 4:7).

Message Point 2: Faith in the Hood (Acts 4:36-37)

Luke indicates that harmony in the hood can produce the by product known as faith in the hood. Barnabus sold a field he owned and brought the money to the apostles' feet. He did this because he was a believer whose heart and mind had been changed such that his value system reflected that of what Jesus represented and promoted throughout His ministry. Barnabus gave little or no thought to addressing his own needs, but rather he submitted his will to the needs of the broader community. Barnabus had faith in the hood. He sought to address the needs of everyone else as exemplified by Jesus. We who are Christians believe that we are our brothers and sisters' keeper.

Message Point 3: Fear in the Hood (Acts 5:1–11)

Just as there is faith in the hood, there is also fear in the hood. Ananias and his wife Sapphira also sold a piece of property but they kept part of what they received for themselves. Then, when they were confronted by the Holy Spirit, they lied. They gave the impression that they had given their all. Often we fear that our needs will not be met. We fear that God will not come through in providing for our needs. So, we go back to how we made it before, sometimes not realizing that we have replaced our faith with fear. In so doing, we suffer the consequences and never live a full and blessed life. Both Ananias and his wife died as a result of their fear of replacing their faith. Thus, they never lived a full life that encompassed all God had for them both individually and personally. How sad it would be to die never realizing that your fear in trusting God limited your capacity to lived the life God had ordained for you.

THAT'LL PREACH

There was a boy; he was small in stature, but he had a desire to play baseball. He would seek out games being played in his neighborhood. Sometimes he would leave one game and go to another. Every time he would go to bat, he would strikeout. Finally, one day, he decided to give up and not look for any more games. Then an older man in the neighborhood saw him and asked him why hadn't he seen him play recently. The boy told him that he was tired of striking out and being laughed at. The old man told the boy, "Your heart and mind have to meet and agree that the goal can be accomplished. And when they meet, faith will produce the first hit." So that we don't fear what God has for us, we must believe that our hearts and minds are in one accord and that God has already provided what we need. All we need to do is believe it and it will come to fruition.

CONCLUSION

As a community of faith, we must believe that God has already given us what we need so that we can be what He calls us to be in our communities. And if we believe that, we can create harmony in our community. Our faith will be seen as a driving factor, and our fears will gradually dissipate. In so doing, we become the beloved community.

NOTES

_____

_____

_____

_____

_____

_____

_____

_____

_____

_____

_____

Playing Favorites

By Dr. Timothy K. Beougher

Lesson Theme	Unit Theme	Scripture
Impartial Love	Godly Love Among Believers	James 2:1-13

INTRODUCTION

We live in a world that tends to judge people based on externals. Our culture says that your worth is determined by the kind of job you have, the kind of car you drive, the kind of house you live in, and the kind of clothes you wear. But the Bible tells us a person's value is not determined by the number of their valuables. James makes clear in our passage for today that while prejudice and favoritism may be commonplace in the world, they have no place in the church.

MESSAGE POINTS

Message Point 1: The Prohibition of Favoritism (James 2:1)

Notice James' reference to "the Lord of glory." He reminds us of the basis for our fellowship with one another. If God brought about our fellowship, we as believers should not break our relationships because of prejudice. The Greek term translated "favoritism" or "partiality" contains a root that means "face." Favoritism is judging others based on appearance, or in other words, at face value. Partiality, judging based on appearance instead of on the basis of the heart, is directly contradictory to the character of God (see 2 Corinthians 5:16). When we see a fellow believer in sin, we care enough about him to approach him in love and point him back to God; that is judging with proper motives. The kind of judging James warns against is a sin: judging with the wrong motive. In this case, we do not have the other person's interests at heart, but our own bias and selfish interests.

Message Point 2: A Picture of Favoritism (vv. 2-4)

Lest anyone think that this is a sin that only others struggle with, James illustrates a situation that each of us can immediately identify with. In the context of a worship service, two different people enter. These individuals are judged based on appearance alone. In ancient times, it was a sign of great wealth and social aristocracy to wear many rings. The culture of that day so valued rings that you could go to stores and rent a ring or two for a special occasion to impress others. Notice the response of the church member, "Here's a good seat for you." Taking the rich man down to the "chief seats" was an attempt to flatter him in hopes of getting something from him (see Matthew 23:6). A second person enters, this one described as a poor man in shabby clothes. The church member is also quick to direct this man to make him stand or sit on the floor. This church member or "usher" is communicating that this person is really not welcome. I wonder if any of us secretly considers ourselves above others. Do we turn away from someone of seeming lesser importance to seek the favor of someone more important? James concludes his illustration in response to this behavior, "Are ye not then partial in yourselves, and are become judges of evil thoughts?" (v. 4).

Message Point 3: The Presumption of Favoritism (vv. 5-7)

Favoritism is to believe that God thinks the same way we think, that God values the same things that we value. First, James tells us that while we may think it is noble to show favoritism, God does not show favoritism on the basis of outward appearance (see Mark 12:14). The believers in James' day needed to hear the message that to follow Christ means to judge by His standards, not on human standards. They needed to be reminded (and so do we) that God chooses the poor in the eyes of the world (see 1 Corinthians 1:26–29). Favoritism presumes that this life is all that matters. If the rich really are in charge, then we would be wise to cater to their every whim. But if Christ is truly the King of kings, the Glorious Lord of the world (and He is), then He, not the rich, deserves our service, our allegiance, and our loyalty. The one who claims to be a follower of the glorious Lord Jesus—but who then shows favoritism—is guilty of having a divided heart, a double mind.

THAT'LL PREACH

Well, Pastor, you say. Pastor, if we can't judge people by their riches, how do we judge them? Should we instead favor the poor and rebuke the rich? No, congregation, that's still judging by outward appearance. Well, Pastor, what standards are we supposed to go by? By God's standards, of course, my sisters and brothers! As James says as he continues this very discourse in verse 14, we will be "judged by the law of liberty." God's law sets us at liberty from the changing and unjust standards of the world and guides us by His holy standards toward heaven.

CONCLUSION

Let's search our hearts for attitudes that don't belong there, attitudes of favoritism or attitudes of prejudice. If we find them there, let's repent of them. Let's ask God to take them away, and to replace them with attitudes of love and compassion as the Lord has commanded. I wonder if people come to mind whom we have not treated properly. We need to restore that relationship with God's help and learn to treat these people differently, according to the merciful law of God.

NOTES

_____

_____

_____

_____

_____

_____

_____

_____

_____

_____

_____

Looking Forward by Looking Backward

By Dr. Timothy K. Beougher

Lesson Theme	Unit Theme	Scripture
Called Through Heritage	The Beginning of a Call	Matthew 1:1-6, 16-17; Hebrews 1:1-5

INTRODUCTION

With every passing year, stores prepare for the Christmas season earlier. They used to wait until December; then they began at Thanksgiving, then at Halloween, and now they begin in mid-summer! Merchants look forward to Christmas with great anticipation. How much more should we worship Him? Just as the genealogy of Jesus Christ helps us anticipate His life on Earth, the study of it can help us celebrate His birth. We can look forward, by looking backward at the lessons we can learn from His family tree. Matthew gives us 42 generations of Jesus' ancestors. As a Hebrew writing for Hebrews, Matthew begins his genealogy with Abraham and follows the line through David to Jesus via Joseph's family, giving us the legal lineage.

MESSAGE POINTS

Message Point 1: God's Grace Displayed in the Lives of Individuals (Matthew 1:1-6)

The story of Christ is the story of grace (John 1:16). In studying Jesus' genealogy, we see some names that surprise us: Tamar (v. 3), a Gentile of questionable actions; Rahab (v. 5), a Gentile and a converted prostitute; Manasseh and Amon (v. 10), who were among the worst kings of Judah. If God would bring the Messianic line through these, He must be a God of grace. Christ was born not to escape our sin, but to deliver us from it. Thus even the foreign and the dishonorable were included in His ancestry. The genealogy of Jesus further contains slaves, psalmists, prophets, kings, miserable failures, and some very ordinary people we don't know much about. We look forward to Christmas by remembering God's grace as displayed in the lives of individuals. His grace is still working wonders in our lives today. No one is too sinful for Christ's blood to cleanse.

Message Point 2: God's Sovereignty Displayed in the Affairs of History (vv. 16-17)

Matthew's record of Jesus' forbearers is carefully divided into three eras of history, each containing 14 names. The first runs from Abraham to David. That was to have been the era of faith, though it was marked by anything but faith. The second era extended from David through Jeconiah. That was to have been the age of royalty under God, but the history of the kings of Judah was anything but royal or godly. The third division covers the period of the captivity of God's Old Testament people, a period of unmitigated failure and misery. Matthew could have listed other descendants, but he put together the Messiah's family tree in three groups to show that all three had equal weight and importance as far as the Messiah is concerned. At the darkest moment of failure, Jesus was born. He became God's perfect Man of Faith, God's Royal King, and the One Who frees all people from their captivity.

Message Point 3: God's Love Displayed in the Fullness of Time (v. 16)

Having given the human lineage of Christ, Matthew is careful to demonstrate that they cannot account for Jesus. Identified with them, He was also separate from them. The process by which Jesus was born is stated differently in Matthew 1:16 from the process by which anyone else in the list of 42 names is born. After 39 uses of the word "beget" or "was the father," Matthew says, "Mary, by whom was born Jesus." This is a subtle difference not brought out in some translations, but it is important. The proclamation in verse 16 is climactic: no human birth, however royal, can account for Jesus. He came by a direct act of God in the fullness of time. Thus we have the mystery of Incarnation—Jesus identified with us, yet is unique from us.

The writer of Hebrews accents this separation of Jesus from us, and even from the angels. The writer can barely find the words to express how immeasurably great Jesus is, saying, "[Jesus] being the brightness of [the Father's] glory, and the express image of his person, and upholding all things by the word of his power, when he had by himself purged our sins, sat down on the right hand of the Majesty on high: Being made so much better than the angels, as he hath by inheritance obtained a more excellent name than they" (Hebrews 1:3-4).

THAT'LL PREACH

When you look back at your family tree, what do you learn? Maybe you learn your uncle shouldn't drink so much. Maybe you learn that your great-great-grandfather was an inventor. Maybe you learn that your ancestors came to this country against their will. No matter what you find in your family tree, you can know that God helped each generation come to the next. God provided for them and protected them so that they could have children, and those children have children, all the way down to you. Now that all that history has come to you, how will you go forward?

CONCLUSION

Looking forward to Christmas? Perhaps this look back will help you look forward. God in grace and mercy does for us what we cannot do. Matthew 1:21 tells us why Jesus came—to save His people from their sins. The best news is that His love and grace are still active today!

NOTES

_____

_____

_____

_____

_____

_____

_____

_____

_____

Who Is He In Yonder Stall?

By Morris Proctor

Lesson Theme	Unit Theme	Scripture
Called Before Birth	The Beginning of the Call	Matthew 1:18-25

INTRODUCTION

An old hymn asks, "Who is He in yonder stall, at whose feet the shepherds fall?" That question and its answer are critical. If we answer incorrectly, we miss our Messiah. We can be mistaken about many things and still enter heaven, but we mustn't be wrong about the baby in the manger. He is the God-man, both human and divine, two complete natures combining in one person. Let's investigate Jesus' deity as discussed in Matthew's account of the Christmas story.

MESSAGE POINTS

Message Point 1: The Virgin Birth Reveals Jesus' Deity (Matthew 1:18)

Matthew states that Mary and Joseph were betrothed. In ancient Israelite culture, parents arranged marriages for their children. When the "engaged" children reached mid-teens, they entered a betrothal period, and it was during this time that Mary became pregnant. There were only two options: either she was a virgin or she was not. Let's assume she was not a virgin. Now we have two more options. Either she had relations with Joseph or with some other man. Nothing we know of Mary indicates unfaithfulness to Joseph, and nothing we know of Joseph indicates he would disclaim responsibility if it were his. If Mary had not been with a man, then she was, in fact, a virgin. How is that possible? When Mary asked that question (Luke 1:34), the angel said: "The Holy Ghost shall come upon thee, and the power of the Highest shall overshadow thee: therefore also that holy thing which shall be born of thee shall be called the Son of God" (v. 35). Son of God is a Hebrew idiom meaning "possessing the nature of God." Without His deity, there is no explanation for the virgin conception and birth.

Message Point 2: The Angel's Words Announce Jesus' Deity (vv. 19-21)

On learning of Mary's pregnancy, Joseph was crushed. But an angel appeared to him saying: "that which is conceived in her is of the Holy Ghost" (v. 20). Literally, it is translated, "out of the Holy Spirit," implying source and substance. The substance or essence of this child is God Himself.

The angel continued: "thou shalt call his name JESUS: for he shall save his people from their sins" (v. 21). The name "Jesus" means "God saves." Jesus' name and mission reveal His deity. Do you recall from algebra class a formula that states, "If A = B and B = C, then A = C"? Jesus is the Savior (1 John 4:14); the only true Savior is God (Isaiah 43:11). Therefore, Jesus is God. Why must Jesus be God to save us? Sin created a penalty, a fair but terrible wage—"For the wages of sin is death" (Romans 6:23). The penalty for sin is eternal. If our Savior were a mere man, how long would He be paying the penalty? Forever. We'd never be saved because the penalty would never be paid. If we're to be saved, we have to have a Savior who can pay an eternal penalty without taking an eternity to do it. Only God Himself can do that.

Message Point 3: Isaiah Predicts Jesus' Deity (vv. 22-23)

Matthew refers to Isaiah 7:14, in which armies attacked the kingdom of Judah led by King Ahaz. Fear gripped Ahaz, and God instructed Isaiah to calm him by allowing him to ask for a sign. When Ahaz refused, Isaiah said, "The Lord himself shall give you a sign; Behold, a virgin shall conceive, and bear a son, and shall call his name Immanuel." God promised that a young woman who currently hadn't known a man would bear a son. Before the boy was old enough to know the difference between good and evil, God would rid Judah of these invaders. The promise was, "Ahaz, when you're afraid, relax and look at the boy, Immanuel. He is a sign that God is with you." Matthew explained that the ultimate fulfillment of Isaiah 7:14 is Jesus Himself. He is a sign God will deliver His people. He is "God with us."

Message Point 4: Joseph's Faith Embraces Jesus' Deity (vv. 24-25)

Hearing the angel, Joseph awakened and obeyed. What faith! It overcame crushed emotions and public ridicule. It overcame physical desire, keeping Mary a virgin until after Christ was born. What could fuel such faith? The fact that this was no ordinary conception. This was miraculous. This was God Himself.

THAT'LL PREACH

In some circles, it's popular to go all out for your baby. You have a formal pregnancy announcement, then a gender reveal party, then a baby shower, then all your monthly baby photoshoots and fancy family photos with matching outfits. Oddly, in some of those same circles, it's popular to be "so done" with Christmas. There's so much argument over when it's ok to start putting up decorations and singing the songs, and it's so commercialized, and there's all that travel in the middle of winter with busy airports. What if we used some of that excitement around babies to celebrate the joy of Christmas? Mary's pregnant; let's celebrate! Joseph just had a dream confirming that it's a boy; let's celebrate! The Wise Men just came to shower the baby with gifts; let's celebrate! Let's celebrate that God Himself has taken on flesh to be "God with us" as a beautiful baby boy, who will save us from our sin!

CONCLUSION

How should we respond to Matthew's Christmas story? Just as Joseph did. With undaunted faith, we are ready to declare our Savior's name. Who is that in yonder stall? He is Jesus, Immanuel, God with us. My God is in yonder stall.

NOTES

_____

_____

_____

_____

_____

_____

_____

The Chosen Ones

By Dr. Daryl Hairston

Lesson Theme	Unit Theme	Scripture
A Regal Response to Holy Light	The Beginning of A Call	Matthew 2:7-15

INTRODUCTION

No one can actually determine their exact path as they meander through seeking to discover their life's purpose. Life will have many turns for every individual with good or bad intentions. Just imagine, Mary as a young girl, starting her life with enthusiasm, dreaming of what she could become, but hesitating because she lived in a time of strict laws. One day she was spontaneously confronted: something caught her attention. Without any warning, she was comforted by an angelic being. "Mary, you will have a child." She was betrothed, "How could this be?" She had not been with her fiancé. Her fiancé was devastated as well upon learning the news. Immediately, there was a conflict with the "upcoming" marriage. He could not process what was happening. God was forming the situation. He has a way to bring together the unimaginable, whether it's through an angel or other means to give comfort and peace to those who are disturbed. There are times when the impossible will fall among you to stretch the very essence of who you are. Just remember, you are a part of the story. What was about to happen could only be a divine intervention that God set up to allow humankind to be a part of something great that will benefit all of humanity. Always be open to God's plan; God just might seek you out and use you.

MESSAGE POINTS

Message Point 1: Facing Opposition (Matthew 2:7-8)

The wise men were commissioned by God to follow specific instructions, but King Herod did not know these instructions. There will always be skeptical moments in life that will question your moral and ethical values. How you handle yourself among others could become an essential seed that will germinate in the midst of opposition to create a change. Stay with God.

The wise men meet King Herod in secret. This was part of God's plan—to have the opposition and the wise men at the meeting—so there will be no excuses when God exposes the outcome. When God initiates a plan, God graciously allows people to carry it out. Whenever you face opposition, there is truly nothing that can distort or take away from what God is developing. Herod learned this as well. Sometimes God will allow all parties, even people like Herod to get involved so that God will get the glory.

Message Point 2: Worship By The Wise Men (vv. 9-12)

God will place His word in the enemy's mouth to send people on their way. "Go search diligently for the child," was the order of the day. God had other plans. The king's voice was heard, the bonds were loosened, and the wise men set out freely to find baby Jesus. Stay the course. God's plan stayed intact as God used astrology to guide them. God guided the wise men straight to where Jesus was. Each assignment is given by God. If we follow the path that God puts us on, we will arrive safely where God will have us. When a plan comes together; you should kneel and worship God with overwhelming joy. Jesus was what the journey was all about. We should give reverence. Then we should offer gifts. The wise men gave him gifts of gold, frankincense, and myrrh. We should offer gifts of service, love, and peace to humanity as we share ourselves fully for the cause of the Kingdom of God. Then God sent them home another way. There are plenty of places to go to tell the story of Jesus. Are you willing to go?

Message Point 3: God's Word Will Come To Fruition (vv. 13-15)

God truly knows how to bring things together. We must be willing to trust our journey to Him while He is unfolding His plan. While going forward with the story; sometimes God will backtrack to make sure that all who were a part of the story are informed. The Angel appeared to Joseph again in a dream and said, "Get up, take the child and his mother and flee to Egypt and remain there until I tell you." Eventually, Herod will be out of the picture. The enemy will always try to stay in the process to harm the very essential things that bring meaning and purpose to humanity. Be of good cheer. God's got this story and God has your life. Follow instructions, carry out the plan, and relax; even if the enemy is searching. The plan belongs to God. Joseph took the mother and the child to Egypt by night; while God took Herod out of the plan. The story will end as God stated. "Out of Egypt I have called my son," and our Savior. Follow the plan, rejoice in the plan, and watch the plan come to fruition.

THAT'LL PREACH

One of the great phenomena of life is trusting the Master at work. We are sometimes hesitant and frustrated with life; we are sometimes on the edge of withering away. Hold on! Allow God to use you for a mighty work. Trust God will win the battle, conquer every journey, and overcome every obstacle. As He tells us in Proverbs 3:5-6, "Trust in the Lord with all your heart and lean not unto your own understanding, in all your ways acknowledge him and he will direct your path."

CONCLUSION

Many days we are faced with decisions that will determine the outcome of many who are struggling in life. God will always be involved as He develops and completes the story. The information you carry can make a difference in miraculous ways. Share God's Word!

NOTES

_____

_____

_____

_____

_____

_____

_____

_____

_____

_____

_____

Proceeding In Purpose!

By Dr. Joshua Mitchell

Lesson Theme	Unit Theme	Scripture
Called to Prepare the Way	The Beginning of a Call	Matthew 3:1-12

INTRODUCTION

In our text, John the Baptist shows an awareness of the limitations of his own power and an awareness of the power of Christ to come. Even though he is not Christ, John faithfully and dutifully plays *his* part in preparing the way for the Messiah to come. In doing so, John teaches us several important lessons around the power of proceeding in our own purposes in concert with the redemptive work of Christ.

MESSAGE POINTS

Message Point 1: The Power of Walking In Purpose (Matthew 3:1-6)

In the text, we find John fully committed to walking in the assignment he has been given. The text implies that John views his purpose as being a mouthpiece for God in Judea: preaching repentance, the willful turning away from sin, to all who would listen, and baptizing them in the Jordan River. And as he operates in his purpose, we learn a few lessons around the power of walking in one's purpose. We first see that John the Baptist pulls some of the power of his own assignment from the prophets of the past. The Gospel writer acknowledges John as the one Isaiah prophesied about (Isaiah 40:3). He is a continuation, if not the manifestation of the prayers and prophecies of his ancestors. And as a result of walking in the purpose in connection to the prophecies and prayers of the past, we see it eventuating in the power to draw people from all around the region to be baptized and confess their sins. This is the power of walking in our purpose—the anointing is attractive!

Message Point 2: The Rebuke of The Righteous (Matthew 3:7-10)

As John walks in his purpose, faithfully preaching and baptizing all who would receive his message of repentance, the power, and people who are drawn to his ministry become a threat to the religious power brokers of the day. The text says that as more and more people are drawn to the work John is doing, these Pharisee and Sadducee religious leaders come spying out John's work—and John stops to rebuke them. He reminds them that they have had the opportunity to repent and that they will not be saved because of their sense of Abrahamic association with God. They would not be pardoned because of the faith of their fore-parents, there is work that *they* would have to do. It is a reminder that as we walk in purpose it may also cause us to rebuke some of the "righteous" within our community who have a critique of our work while not doing their own.

Message Point 3: A Preview of the Promise (Matthew 3:11-12)

After the text, John provides some perspective on his own work in the grand scheme of things that God desires to do for God's people. Despite the large numbers of people coming from "Jerusalem, and all Judaea, and all the region round about Jordan" (v. 5) because of the power of his preaching and the appeal of his baptisms, John explains to the listening crowd of supporters and religious skeptics that what he is providing is just a preview of coming attractions! While John is baptizing them with water for the repentance of sin, John promises that another is coming behind him who will take this baptism to another level. John promises, "I indeed baptize you with water unto repentance… he shall baptize you with the Holy Ghost, and with fire" (v. 11). John reminds us that the exercising of our gifts is not for our own praise but to point to one who is far greater than we are.

THAT'LL PREACH

I am not much of a shopper, but I do enjoy trips to the local mall with my family. While my wife and son are looking for clothes, I make a pilgrimage to my favorite part of the building: the food court. What I enjoy about the food court is that I can walk around, and outside of each food vendor is someone who is providing samples of the food that the vendor provides. At one of my favorite vendors, the workers most regularly say to customers who try the food for the first time: "If you thought *that* was good, there's much more of where that came from!" John reminds us that at our best we are delicious samples of God's power—and that prayerfully when people engage us, we too can say, "If you thought that was good, there's much more where that came from!"

CONCLUSION

Each of us has a role to play in the redemptive work of God on the earth. John's work of preaching and baptizing was powerful work, work that drew people in, and work that caused him to occasionally call people out. But ultimately, John walks in his own purpose to provide a preview (or a sample) of things to come in the power and promise of Jesus Christ.

NOTES

_____

_____

_____

_____

_____

_____

_____

_____

_____

_____

From the Ground Up

By Dr. Matthew C. Jones

Lesson Theme	Unit Theme	Scripture
Called to Proclaim	Jesus and Calls in His Ministry	Luke 4:14-22

INTRODUCTION

In the early 1990s, Daymond John and a group of his friends were working on an idea for a new clothing line that would reflect and give back to their community. They tirelessly labored in Daymond's garage creating designs and then went public with a product—a batch of 80 hats—which sold-out on the streets of Queens, New York. The hats were well received, so the group went back to designing and producing more products. In need of capital, Daymond mortgaged his home for money to build the company FUBU from the ground up. It went on in the late '90s to become a great success and as they say, the rest is history. There is something about this starting from the bottom that moves us, especially when it is aimed to serve the underprivileged and underrepresented. With this in mind, we turn to Luke 4 and think of how this Jewish man—Jesus Christ—in a place of marginalization began something new for His people, Israel. Unlike FUBU, His product would never expire, because Jesus came to give everlasting life and make disciples who would know the power of the Spirit and the potency of Scripture, in the face of the pressure of society to the end of the ages (Matthew 28:19-20).

MESSAGE POINTS

Message Point 1: The Power of the Spirit (Luke 4:14-15)

Jesus' public ministry really gets going in the fourth chapter of Luke. Jesus builds His company from the ground up in Galilee (v. 14) and then goes to His familiar childhood stomping grounds of Nazareth (v. 16). To succeed in His mission, Jesus gave His life for the work of discipleship, He offered the prophesied Kingdom of God to Israel. To prove His kingdom credentials as the long-awaited Messiah, in Luke 4 we read of Jesus coming "in the power of the Spirit" (v. 14), just after He was publicly ordained by the Spirit (3:22). This work of the Spirit did not originate here; all through chapters 1-3, the Spirit was moving in witnesses to testify Jesus was indeed the Christ. More uniquely and intimately, Luke tells us about how the Spirit was used by the Father in the incarnation of the eternal Son (1:35) who became the man Jesus.

Message Point 2: The Potency of the Scripture (vv. 16-21)

Jesus substantiated His identity in the prophesied signs and statements of the Hebrew Bible. This is one of the reasons teaching was so important to Him because it corroborated that He was the figure the sacred text predicted. In Luke 4:17-19, Jesus used Isaiah 61:1–2 and 58:6 to proclaim His identity. In His presence, we read the "eyes of all" were "fixed on him" (v. 20) and Jesus told the people, "This day is this scripture fulfilled" (v. 21). Hearing this, Luke tells us Nazareth was "speaking well of him" (v. 22), just as the Galilean crowds did earlier when He was "praised by all" (v. 15). The Scripture proved itself to be truly potent, accomplishing its purpose (Isaiah 40:8, 55:10–11, Hebrews 4:12).

Message Point 3: The Pressure of Society (v. 22)

In verse 22, we hear uncertainty forming as some ask, "Is this not Joseph's son?" New Testament scholars take this to be an expression of distrust. Although His words were powerful and the people admitted it, they still responded by looking down on Jesus' family background via His stepfather Joseph. We know from the Gospel accounts and historical data there was a good deal of prejudice in that culture toward those who came from Nazareth (see John 1:46), so the pressure was on as Jesus' ministry was getting off the ground. He would be attacked not only for his message and divinity but also socially for his neighborhood and family. Nazareth was a ghetto to many, so the thought of the Messiah being from this place would have scandalized the cultural powers of the elite.

THAT'LL PREACH

In the hit song "In the Ghetto," hip hop artist Rakim observes, "it ain't where you're from, it's where you're at." The antagonists of Jesus were so concerned with where Jesus was from that they missed where He was going. They failed not only to hear his message but even more tragically his critics failed to see the cross. In terms of His teaching, as Luke 4 continues, Jesus goes on to tell His audience two back-to-back biblical accounts about the God of Israel giving compassion to ethnic foreigners (see Luke 4:23–27), which resulted in the crowd being "filled with rage" (v. 28), driving Jesus out of the city, and trying to kill him (v. 29). The context is clear that they did not want a lowly Jewish messiah from the outskirts kicking off his company from the ground up with other marginalized folks. With this in mind, we can say they missed the gift from the ghetto, that is, the eternal Son in the flesh offering His kingdom of peace.

CONCLUSION

In Luke 4, the launch of Jesus' ministry is documented by the historian for his readers to see how it all began from the ground up. In the redemptive storyline of the Bible, Jesus the incarnate Son appears at the perfect timing of the Father (cf. Galatians 4:4), as the Spirit led Him into the humble start of His earthly work. Jesus called the lost to Himself and made disciples, whom He died for on the Cross, laying the foundation for His church in His sacrifice and saturating it with the preaching of the Scripture. By His resurrection, He conquered sin and death, extending not only forgiveness to His followers but also power for life by the Spirit. Our Lord did all of this in the face of the hostilities of the world, which He willingly faced as He built (and continues to build!) His church for the glory of His Father to the ends of the earth. Amen.

NOTES

_____

_____

_____

_____

_____

_____

_____

Dead Fish

By John Burton, Jr.

Lesson Theme	Unit Theme	Scripture
Called to Significance	Jesus and Calls in His Ministry	Luke 5:1-11

INTRODUCTION

Cod, sole, sea bass, salmon, and halibut are just a few of the variety of fish that can be purchased from merchants at the famous Fisherman's Wharf in San Francisco. Held at one of California's greatest tourist attractions, its history goes back to Italian and Chinese immigrants who chose fishing as a trade to capitalize on the population boom happening with the gold rush in the area during the early 1900s. In small boats, they set out to make a living catching fish and the now-famous Dungeness crab. To catch something means that it's usually alive. Although the fish purchased at the wharf are dead, they are considered fresh. Fish that have been dead for days or not properly preserved possess a foul stench. It is easily detectable after one whiff. Jesus' lesson in our text is to demonstrate how to catch dead people who are alive. Although the disciples were following Jesus, they were most likely walking dead spiritually, because they had yet to fully commit themselves to Him. Jesus provides Peter on-the-job training that changes his entire idea of the practice of fishing.

MESSAGE POINTS

Message Point 1: Jesus Sets the Setting (Luke 5:1-3)

In the area of real estate, one word is key: location, location, location. Establishing the proper setting aids in the compelling nature of what is trying to be conveyed. It sets the tone of how people react, how information could be received, and possibly the background of those around. Jesus selected the Sea of Gennesaret. He noticed Simon Peter, and most likely Andrew, James, and John busy washing their nets. This was a familiar setting for these commercial fishermen. Jesus decided to climb into Simon Peter's boat and request he pull slight away from shore for Him to conduct His teaching to the growing crowd. Although this would seem like an odd request, Jesus and the disciples had a familiarity. It was this familiarity that Jesus used to His advantage. Jesus is all-knowing and He knew where the disciples would be. Although they were called to follow Him, He decided to show up where they were. Jesus shows up in familiar places in our lives. Just like the disciples, when we don't seek to find Him, He is still aware of where we are physically and spiritually. When we seek to lose ourselves in the world and with the familiar, God still shows up unexpectedly where we are to remind us He is still here waiting on us.

Message Point 2: Jesus Teaches the Session (vv. 4-7)

In our school years, one of the best feelings was when the teacher stopped talking and class was over. This signified the lesson was done. When Jesus finished speaking to the multitude, He still had more He wanted to teach. He commands Simon Peter to "let down your nets for a draught" (v. 4). This was not a recommendation but a command. Simon Peter offers Jesus this tiresome and expert fisherman commentary on behalf of his crew, "Master, we have toiled all the night, and have taken nothing: nevertheless at thy word I will let down the net" (v. 5) Interestingly, Jesus does not respond. Once the nets are lowered, they fill to the point of almost tearing.

Jesus' unique teaching method proves they did not know better. Simon Peter's "What do you know?" attitude is challenged and defeated. Our experience, no matter how vast, is no match for the Master. Why do we even challenge an all-knowing God? He knows the plans He has for us, which are good and not of evil to provide us with a wonderful future with hope (Jeremiah 29:11). When we trust Him, He can do more than what we could think or imagine on our best day (Ephesians 3:20). Our miracle could be on the way if we'd just stop and listen to the teacher.

Message Point 3: The Disciples Concede to Submission (vv. 8-11)

When Simon Peter sees what Jesus has done, he falls to his knees to repent, "Depart from me; for I am a sinful man, O Lord" (v. 8). Simon Peter's surrender signifies two things: his wrongdoing and Jesus Christ's Lordship. The blessing allows him to see Jesus and himself through a new lens. Simon Peter's skepticism caused him to know he was not worthy to be in the presence of Christ's greatness. His verbal conversion is similarly signified by the changing of Jesus' title of Master to Lord. All the while his comrades say nothing but are equally amazed. Jesus ignores Simon Peter's confession completely. He simply tells him "Fear not," but going forward "thou shalt catch men" (v. 10). Was the fear of the blessing, the resigning of the job completely, or of Jesus Himself? No one knows but they follow His command, leave everything, and follow Him. Following Jesus always requires relinquishing of your will for His will to be done (Luke 22:42). What are you holding on to?

THAT'LL PREACH

In a world inundated by robocalls and pop up ads, we are often left to wonder, "What's the catch?" Sadly, society has conditioned us to be a community of skeptics, that we question any and almost everything. We're overly cautious and doubtful of certain validity. When it seems too good to be true, we tend to believe that it usually is. We become worried that there are hidden problems associated with it. However, with Jesus, He is the real thing! His ways and opportunities are divinely better than our own (Isaiah 55:8-9). All He desires is that we trust Him completely and not half-heartedly. He is the God of the universe. Everything there is, He made. So why not trust Him? Although it may seem fishy to you, trust God and do the spiritual sniff test.

CONCLUSION

Do you smell it? Again, dead things carry a stench. It goes completely undetected to many, except for those who are spiritually aware. It's this awareness that God desires that we are sensitive to and not sanitized from. Spiritually dead fish are always around but it takes an expert fisher to detect when, what, where, and how to catch them. The prophet Ezekiel teaches us dead things can live again (Ezekiel 37). Through the practice of fishing, Jesus changed these fishermen's business sense. Are you about your Father's business or your own? Be committed to catching people for Christ. Cast your net!

NOTES

_____

_____

_____

_____

_____

Abiding In The Presence of the Lord

By Dr. Michael K. Roussell

Lesson Theme		Unit Theme		Scripture
Called to Heal		Jesus and Calls in His Ministry		Mark 2:1-12

INTRODUCTION

Do you see a need for a change in your life? In your home? On your job? No matter what you face in life, you can be victorious in His presence. Remember that God will provide all the strength, power, and wisdom you need if you ask Him. It's yours for the asking as you abide in His presence. Let us keep our expectations high, regardless of our circumstances, by praying more, believing God for healing. Also, I pray that we maintain a proper reverence for God as we abide in His presence.

The Gospel of Mark is full of the power and presence of God. Mark has a way of telling how being in the presence of the Lord changes lives. In this passage, we see Jesus, after entering into Capernaum, go into a house. The word spread that Jesus was there until there was no more room left in the house. It was then that He began to preach the Word of God to the people that were there. In our text, three things happen while in His presence.

MESSAGE POINTS

Message Point 1: You Gain Wisdom In The Presence of The Lord (Mark 2:3)

When we use the phrase "in the presence of God" we are talking about time spent with the Lord or time spent in His Word. Prayer, wisdom, hope, healing, deliverance, freedom, meditation, and more are all found in His presence. What is wisdom? Wisdom is the ability to make the right decision at the right time. While Jesus was in the house at Capernaum, a group of people brought a man that needed healing and lowered him down to Jesus. The man who was sick with palsy was healed by Jesus. Certainly, they made the right decision at the right time.

Message Point 2: We Can Expect Jesus To Answer Prayers While In His Presence (v. 5)

We as Christians should live a life of expectation every day. Do you have any confidence in Him? Has your confidence grown lately? The Word of God says, "Let us therefore come boldly unto the throne of grace, that we may obtain mercy, and find grace to help in a time of need" (Hebrews 4:16). Mark 11:23 tells us that when we pray, we are to believe. Does this describe you? The text states that Jesus gave them their request when they went to Him.

We must pray and come to Jesus until our confidence in Him becomes stronger. When was the last time you did that? We must remember that God always answers prayer. Sometimes He says "yes," "no," or "wait." However, let's pray regularly. Let's expect God to answer our prayers by thanking Him in advance. Let's watch how we talk after we pray. Let's not do anything contrary to our prayers. Jesus can do miraculous things if we abide in His presence!

Message Point 3: There Is Healing In The Presence of the Lord (v. 12)

In Mark 2 we find that God is a Healer (v. 12). We know that Jesus is "the LORD that healeth thee" (Exodus 15:26). Healing was purchased in the atonement. We have a promise from Almighty God regarding restoring our health. Furthermore, God still heals today. Although He may not heal everyone, I have spoken with many people who have been healed of sickness and disease. Let us examine our hearts. Let us call upon the elders of the church. Let us stand on the promises of God. Let's continue to speak the word of faith. Let's increase our meditation on God's Word. Let us continue to abide in His presence and expect wondrous things. In Jesus Name!

THAT'LL PREACH

A few years ago I had the privilege of speaking with a man who was on the 80th floor of the World Trade Center when an airplane crashed into it. This attack on America is known as 9/11. He was in his office at the time. In talking with Him, I found that he was a praying man who believed in the Lord Jesus Christ before this incident happened. While in his office on that day, he looked up and saw the plane coming directly toward the building. However, the man's life was miraculously saved. He explained how he got down under his desk as he saw the plane approaching. After the plane struck the building, there was a man with a flashlight in his hand, who appeared out of nowhere, which led him to safety. This man saved his life. To this day, he does not know who the man was. He believes it was an angel and that he was in the presence of the Lord. Without a doubt, God's presence was certainly with this man as he was led to safety.

CONCLUSION

After seeing the benefits of God from being in His presence, what are you going to do? Wisdom, answers, healing, and what's more: peace, deliverance, freedom, and power are all yours as you abide in His presence. The songwriter wrote, "What a friend we have in Jesus; All our sins and griefs to bear. What a privilege to carry, everything to God in prayer." Lord, I thank You for Your Word. Forgive me for not taking the time to spend in Your presence. Help me increase my time with You. In Jesus Name!

NOTES

_____

_____

_____

_____

_____

_____

_____

_____

Protected, Sanctified, and Glorified

By Michael D. Goolsby

Lesson Theme	Unit Theme	Scripture
Called as the Intercessor	Jesus and Calls in His Ministry	John 17:14–24

INTRODUCTION

There are a number of instances throughout the Gospels where Jesus prays about circumstances and occasions. He is earnest, sincere, and reverent in every petition raised to His Father, in every prayer. This being so, there is no denying a distinction in this prayer, here in John 17, owed to Jesus' passionate affections for His Father, as well as for those the Father had given Him. This, of course, pertains to Jesus' disciples, which includes those of us who follow Jesus in our own day and time. Many consider this prayer of Jesus for His followers throughout all time to be His most in-depth, passionate, zealous appeal to His Father of any other prayer He prayed. This is a difficult claim to make of Jesus, the very Son of God, when every prayer He prayed possesses the same preeminent value, owing to who He is. Yet this prayer in John 17 does claim some distinction. It seems to be his most desperate prayer, prayed most passionately, appealing to his Father for every provision, for all those His blood has redeemed. Let this prayer from our Savior give us full assurance of every provision His petition and His blood has claimed.

MESSAGE POINTS

Message Point 1: The Word and the Hatred of the World (John 17:14-16)
In this passage, Jesus affirms to His Father that He had obediently given His Father's Word to those the Father had given to Him: the disciples. The Father's Word, empowered by His Spirit, is the most useful, effective resource the disciples could possess. This is true for us in our day as well.

Yet, as wonderful of a message as this is, the Gospel, and those who announce it are fiercely hated by Satan and those he has deceived. This is why Jesus pleads with his Father, to "keep them from the evil one." He doesn't ask His Father to remove them from the world, as He had commissioned them to proclaim His saving Word to the world. What Jesus requests of His Father is that He keeps them from the evil one. That the Father keeps them from being enmeshed in the schemes and traps of the devil because those traps would make them unfit for the work for which He had commissioned them. The Father has faithfully commissioned us to this work today, He has, therefore, enabled His beloved saints, and keeps us in this work.

Message Point 2: Sanctification of His Disciples (vv. 17-21)
Along with being kept by the Father, He wanted them to be dedicated to the special purpose of laying the groundwork for the mission of the Gospel. In verses 17-21, Jesus petitions His Father that He would "sanctify" the ones His Father had given to Him.

To be sanctified is to be set aside for a particular purpose. A particular surgical instrument is set aside in an operating room for a particular surgical procedure. It alone has the unique design and function for the specific kind of surgery needed. In the same way, the early disciples were called and designated to carry out the unique mission of proclaiming the message of the Gospel for all who would hear and receive it. This is true for us today too who are called Jesus' disciples. Jesus prayed for our sanctification as well.

We have been sanctified, that is "made holy" by God's Spirit, to live in obedience to Him, reflecting His image in the world around us to draw others to salvation through the Gospel.

Message Point 3: Jesus Gives Us His Glory (vv. 22-24)

In these last verses of this message, Jesus lifts up to His Father an amazingly glorious request. He asks that His disciples would share His glory. Wow! What a remarkable request this is!

He showed us His glory first in our redemption. In calling us to himself through the Gospel to become His own and possess all the treasures of salvation for all the eternal ages, He gives a most glorious display of His presence in our lives (John 3:16). Being filled with His Spirit, who joins with our spirits affirming that we are indeed God's children, displays Christ's glory to us (Romans 8:16–17). He blesses us with every spiritual blessing in the heavenly places making us "holy and without blame before him," making known His glory (Ephesians 1:4). Our hearts should overflow with gratefulness for this glorious petition of our blessed Savior.

THAT'LL PREACH

This brings to mind, the ending of the apostle Paul's prayer in verses 20 and 21 of Ephesians chapter 3, where he said, "Now unto him that is able to do exceeding abundantly above all that we ask or think, according to the power that worketh in us, Unto him be glory in the church by Christ Jesus throughout all ages, world without end. Amen."

Jesus' petition of His Father to give us His glory is a resounding agreement that He will indeed do "exceeding abundantly above all that we ask or think." Paul's words make clear why Jesus would make such a request of his Father. If God does more for us than we can imagine, what will He do for Jesus?

CONCLUSION

To remind ourselves of the glorious gift the word of God truly is, all we need do is recall Jesus is the full expression of the life-giving message of God, intended for a world in need of the Spirit-empowered truth, that sets men free! All that Jesus said to His disciples during His time with them, they recorded for the succeeding generations, of all who would come to know Christ through what they had written. That includes us, beloved. What Jesus said to God in this prayer applies to us today. Christ has prayed that we would be protected. He has prayed that we would be sanctified. And He has prayed that we would see His glory. Let us eagerly work as we look forward to this reward!

NOTES

_____

_____

_____

_____

God's Prophetic Women

By Porsha Williams

Lesson Theme	Unit Theme	Scripture
Prophesying Daughters	The Call of Women	Luke 2:36-38; Acts 2:16-21, 21:8-9

INTRODUCTION

Have you ever visited a church, looked around, and wondered, "Where are the women in leadership?" Why are churches filled with men at the helm of the leadership? For centuries, there has been much debate over women serving in ministry and in what capacities they are allowed to serve. In some denominations and faith traditions, women are not allowed to be ordained, preside over the ordinances in worship, or preach. Women have been disregarded as second-class and unfit to minister within some church contexts because leaders have taken Scripture readings out of context. However, the Biblical texts for today are evidence that God is indeed calling women to speak prophetically in the public square. In our reading for today, we see three New Testament examples of women ministering prophetically.

MESSAGE POINTS

Message Point 1: Prophesying Women know no age limits (Luke 2:36-38)

Age tends to play a role in who can speak and who cannot. These rules did not apply to Anna. God had called Anna to be a prophet. Anna, who was widowed, older in age, and no longer under the protection of any man, would have been considered to be an outsider during this time. Yet, Anna prophesied anyhow. She was at least eighty-four years old at the time that we meet her in the text. Anna was consistent with being in the Temple, and she fasted and prayed continually. Anna could be found worshiping both day and night. She was the one who shared alongside Simeon about little Jesus and how he would be the one who would bring about redemption to all of Jerusalem. That was bold for Anna to say, which would have required conviction and a high level of confidence in God. Anna could have been dismissed for her age, yet she pressed on and shared anyhow. Anna could have been home, laying low and resting as many who are elderly would, but she decides to keep on pressing and speaking. When we are called to do prophetic work, it is a life long commitment that continues to show our faithfulness even as we age.

Message Point 2: Women were destined to be prophetic (Acts 2:16-21)

The idea of women prophesying did not begin with the New Testament. Women had been declared to be prophetic and expected to be prophetic since the ancient times of the early prophets, especially the prophet Joel. Peter stands up in front of a crowd on the day of Pentecost and proclaims that Joel stated God will pour out God's Spirit "upon all flesh" and that both men and women will prophesy. This pouring of spirit was not limited to one particular kind of person. The Spirit of the Lord was intended for all to have access. Scripture has been fulfilled on the day of Pentecost as the Holy Spirit makes its arrival as a great comforter. God had spoken about this long before the life and times of Jesus. Therefore, women were destined to be prophetic. It was always in God's plans for it to be so.

Message Point 3: Martial status does not determine prophetic ability (Acts 21:8-9)

Just as Anna was widowed and unmarried, the daughters of Philip the Evangelist were also unmarried. There is a notion that leadership must be married to serve. Luke, the writer of Acts tells us that this is untrue. The daughters of Philip were unmarried women. The four of them were living at home with their father in Caesarea. Their father had been serving as one of the seven evangelists. These daughters knew that there was work to be done in the spreading and sharing of the Gospel of Jesus, the Risen Savior. In order to do this, these daughters had to be secure in who they were as women under the protection of their father. In these times, the women were under their father's protection, and he would have the social authority to say whether or not they were able to speak. Philip did not hinder his daughters from prophesying as the Spirit would move them to speak. If these women were seen as "outspoken," their eligibility for marriage might have suffered, but Philip was not concerned with that. He allowed them to move as God would have them, which tells that Philip was supportive of God calling his daughters to the prophetic work of local ministry even when unmarried.

THAT'LL PREACH

Over the last few years, with the rise of Black Lives Matter and the #MeToo Movement, we have seen even more women in the forefront and on the lines of social justice. Women have been empowered at the polls and in protest. When we consider the work of the prophetic in today's context, we see more women speaking truth to power. Now is the time for the daughters to prophesy and to work their prophetic gifting. The biblical text shows us that prophetic women have been present since the ancient days, and they are not going anywhere. From Deborah and Jael to the women at the tomb to proclaim that Jesus has risen, prophetic women are always in season carrying the Good News of the Gospel of Jesus.

CONCLUSION

Womanist theologians and practitioners have begun using the phrase, "If not for the women" as a salute to the foremothers that have paved the way for womanist work and scholarship. Womanism recognizes the accomplishments of women of color who have trail-blazed for the whole of the community. Today we can acknowledge that for the Black church if it had not been for the women pushing the ministries forward, the church would not be what it is and where it is. If it had not been for the women of ancient days, the foundation of the church universal would not be where it is. God has been utilizing the gifts of women and calling women into the forefront—regardless of age, marital status, and class—to push the Gospel forward.

NOTES

_____

_____

_____

_____

_____

_____

_____

A Life-Giving Message from an Unlikely Messenger

By Pastor Tommy E. Smith, Jr.

Lesson Theme	Unit Theme	Scripture
Called to Evangelize	The Call of Women	John 4:25-42

INTRODUCTION

By today's standards, the first-century world was greatly lacking in appreciating the talents and abilities of women. This is evident from what we know of historical practices, as well as the art and literature of that time. Even the Bible itself is fairly patriarchal in the customs it describes and the language it uses. However, one significant exception to this is Jesus. Jesus went out of His way to be more inclusive toward women in His ministry. This is not to say that He was a feminist crusader, but He did often feature women in prominent roles in His parables and stories. One real-life example of this occurs with His encounter with the Samaritan woman at the well of Sychar. This encounter may seem inconsequential at first glance, but a closer look lets us know that Jesus bestowed a very high honor on this woman by allowing her to play a key role in the evangelization of her community, and in setting a model for many missionary efforts to follow!

MESSAGE POINTS

Message Point 1: Messiah is Coming! (John 4:25–26)

The encounter that Jesus had with this woman at the well of Sychar was highly unusual for more than one reason. In addition to the fact that she was a female engaging in discussion, she also was a Samaritan. While one can argue that the inequity women were subjected to at that time was not intentionally mean-spirited, this definitely was not the case with Samaritans. There was outright animosity between Samaritans and Jews. Yet this woman and Jesus had been carrying on a civil discussion of a volatile topic for some time; that is until the subject of her sin was broached. She then wanted to change the subject to something less personal, i.e. which mountain is holier, yours or ours! After Jesus corrected her on this point, she countered that they will just have to wait for the Messiah to arrive and reveal the answer to the mystery. Jesus then said to her words that must have exploded like a bombshell, "I who speak to you am he!"

Message Point 2: The Urgent Need for Evangelization (vv. 27–38)

Upon hearing this news, the woman excitedly ran to tell the townsfolk about the stranger she met at the well (forgetting all about the water pot that brought her to the well in the first place!). As she leaves, the disciples return from an errand and encourage Him to eat something. Jesus explains that He has another, the spiritual source of nourishment, and He uses this moment to give an object lesson on the importance of and need for evangelization. As He so often does, He uses a parable to make His point. He describes the world and the people on it as ripe and ready to be harvested. It takes much labor to bring a crop to the point of harvesting: planting, cultivating, and reaping. He tells His disciples that others have done the hard work of sowing, but they have been blessed with the opportunity to reap souls for eternal life—by sharing the good news of the Gospel! This is the essence of the work of evangelization, and all who are called to such labor are highly blessed of God.

Message Point 3: The Life-Changing Effects of Evangelism! (vv. 39-42)

The story now switches back to the Samaritan village of Sychar. This woman, who in all likelihood had an unsavory reputation due to her questionable past, was suddenly unafraid to bring to others a religious message. She was personally convinced of Jesus' identity as the Messiah due to the conversation she had with Him, and her convictions allowed her to share this news with boldness and without shame. This affected the townsfolk enough to invite Jesus to stay with them for two days. At the end of this time, the people no longer had to take this woman's word for who Jesus was. They were convinced through their own interactions with Him that He was indeed the Messiah! Retrospectively, the beauty of God's symphonic coordination in this incident is extraordinary. Jesus has a conversation with a marginalized woman from a despised minority about His universal saving grace, and she goes on to be the messenger to spark the conversion of her entire previously ostracized village—all while the apostles were out grocery shopping!

THAT'LL PREACH

It's one thing to get information from a third party, but it's quite another to experience it first-hand. The people in this Samaritan village were willing to entertain Jesus based on what their neighbor told them, but after directly experiencing Him for themselves, they wholeheartedly accepted Him. This is not unlike the process that our greatest universities use to train scientists. Students are required to attend lecture classes where they are taught various theories and concepts, but the process doesn't end there. The lectures are followed up by laboratory classes, where quantities are measured, data is taken, mistakes are made, and results are proven. Consequently, the information students received in lectures has been transformed from abstract theoretical ideas into tangible reality. God accomplishes the same transformation within all who are willing to go from merely hearing about Jesus of Nazareth to accepting and experiencing Him as our Lord and Savior, Jesus Christ!

CONCLUSION

Jesus did not come to earth to right all of the sociological wrongs in Jewish or Roman society. However, he did espouse truths and undertake actions that began the process of chipping away at some of the more odious social practices of that time. His parable of the Good Samaritan, His conversation with the Samaritan woman at the well, and His commissioning of Mary to tell the disciples that He is risen on that first Easter morning are all examples of subtle and not so subtle actions that helped to eventually make society more equitable for all. We can pay homage to these acts by continuing the tradition of mutual respect and inclusivity that He set in motion.

NOTES

_____

_____

_____

_____

_____

_____

_____

Jesus Embraces Women in His Ministry

By CaReese Mukulu

Lesson Theme	Unit Theme	Scripture
Mary Magdalene: A Faithful Disciple	The Call of Women	Luke 8:1–3; Mark 15:40; John 20:10–18

INTRODUCTION

At first glance, the Gospels seem centered on men. We need not take this to mean that women were absent or unimportant. The culture of the first century Israel was vastly different from that of 21st century America. Women had few rights and were seen as less than their male counterparts.

In some ways, Jesus broke with the tradition in His regard for women. Jesus demonstrated compassion and treated women with respect. He included women in teaching illustrations and parables. He also ministered to women by offering forgiveness, deliverance, and healing. Jesus welcomed women and taught them alongside the men. After the Resurrection, women were the first to see the risen Christ and were present with the other disciples when Matthias was chosen to replace Judas. Finally, women are equal recipients of the Holy Spirit's gifts (Acts 2:17–18).

In the culture of first-century Israel many had a low view of women but based on His treatment of women, Jesus did not share this view. In this way, Jesus established a new standard for the Church to follow—one in which women have the same rights, privileges, and responsibilities as men to serve Him wholeheartedly.

In this lesson, we will visit several scenes where Mary Magdalene shows her devotion to the Lord. We see Mary included in the life of Jesus at the high points as well as the low points.

MESSAGE POINTS

Message Point 1: Traveling with Jesus (Luke 8:1–3)

While Capernaum served as the base for Jesus' ministry, He traveled to nearby towns to teach and bring the power of God. In addition to the Twelve, Jesus brought several women that were associated with His ministry. These women were not simply for show. They took part in providing for Jesus and His entourage. It was not unusual at that time for women to share their wealth with rabbis. However, it was unusual for women to travel with a rabbi. Jesus was probably met with criticism for breaking with the accepted convention. Jesus sets a new standard by creating a place for women in His ministry.

Mary is among the women traveling with Jesus. Luke, the physician, makes sure the reader keeps Mary's history in mind. Jesus had freed Mary Magdalene from demonic possession in the past. In so doing, Luke highlights the remarkable transformation of Mary Magdalene. She begins as a prisoner of demons. As we shall see, Mary goes on to be the bearer of His word to the Disciples.

Message Point 2: Faithful to the End (Mark 15:40)

Mark also notes that the women traveled with Jesus and provided for His ministry. He mentions that the women are eyewitnesses to Jesus' crucifixion and goes on to identify some of the women by name: Mary Magdalene, Mary the mother of James, and Salome the mother of James and John. These women were eyewitnesses to the crucifixion as well as the burial of Jesus. Mark's specific mention is a testament to the love and devotion of these women. The devotion of the women clearly exceeded that of the men, as the Eleven had already deserted Him. The disciples claimed that they would die for Jesus, but in Jesus' darkest hour, only the women remained. Mary Magdalene was counted among the faithful.

Message Point 3: Proclaiming the Good News (John 20:10–18)

Jesus' first Resurrection appearance was to Mary Magdalene, from whom He had cast seven demons (Luke 8:2). Like Mary, Peter, and John had come to the tomb. They looked inside and then left. John also notes that Mary was present at Jesus' death and came to the tomb early Sunday morning.

The account of Mary's encounter with Jesus is touching. She is clearly overcome with grief. She carries on a conversation with the angels sitting in the tomb without consolation. When Jesus appears, she doesn't recognize Him. She proceeds to tell Him of her grief. Only when He speaks her name does Mary recognize Jesus.

Scholars note the significance of Jesus' first appearance. Rather than appearing to Pilate, Caiaphas, or one of the disciples, Jesus appeared to Mary. It's an indication of His affection for her and it strengthens the historicity of the account. If the account had been invented, no Jewish author would have chosen a woman to be the first to see the resurrected Christ. Perhaps most significantly, Mary was given the responsibility of reporting what she had seen: the risen Christ. This duty Mary carried out faithfully.

THAT'LL PREACH

A good transformation is irresistible. Television networks are full of shows featuring houses fallen into disrepair that are later discovered and transformed into beautiful homes by skilled designers and builders. Properties that had previously been written off suddenly become very valuable.

People undergo transformations as well. Home transformations are amazing, but they do not compare to the incredible transforming work of God in the lives of His people. God takes people in any condition and His power can make even the most undesirable characters into powerful vessels of His love and grace.

CONCLUSION

First-century Israel undervalued women in several ways. Though the methods are different, 21st century America can also make women believe they are "less than." While women enjoy many legal rights, women are often made to feel "less than" if they don't look a certain way, have a certain relationship status, or have a certain family situation. Now, as then, Jesus comes against these lies with the truth: women are valued. Women are important. Women are included in the Kingdom of God and the ministry of Jesus.

NOTES

_____

_____

_____

_____

Going Out and Bringing In

By Beth Potterveld

Lesson Theme	Unit Theme	Scripture
Priscilla: Called to Minister	The Call of Women	Acts 18:1–3, 18–21, 24–26; Romans 16:3–4

INTRODUCTION

Priscilla and Aquila were kicked out of Rome. Emperor Claudius wanted to stop what he saw the riotous bickering of the "Jews" in Rome. (At this time, few outside the faith understood the difference between Christianity and Judaism.) So he banished them from the capital. He didn't try to dig into the issues or sort out peace in his city. He just pushed people out. Priscilla and Aquila saw this; they were directly affected by it. We see that they moved over 700 miles because of it. Were they bitter? Did they turn Claudius's example back at him? No. They were hospitable. Their hospitality brought people in. They brought people into their work, the right belief, and their home.

MESSAGE POINTS

Message Point 1: Bring People into Work (Acts 18:1–3)

In our first verses, we are introduced to Priscilla and Aquila. They are Jewish Christians who had been outcast from Rome and settled in Corinth. We can imagine that the move was not easy. They had to establish themselves and their work in a completely different city hundreds of miles from their former home, simply because the Emperor didn't want them around. Even though Priscilla and Aquila are new to the area themselves, they welcome Paul as he travels to Corinth from the other direction, from Athens to the west. Paul is at that time without many of his traveling companions and knows nobody in Corinth. But he quickly becomes friends and co-workers with Priscilla and Aquila because they share not only their faith but also their craft. With no one to recommend Paul to them, Priscilla and Aquila still bring Paul into work with them so he can support himself as he preaches to the Corinthian church. Having just experienced that feeling of uprootedness themselves, Priscilla and Aquila quickly see Paul suffering the same, and reach out to bring him in, to work with them.

Message Point 2: Bring People into Right Belief (vv. 24–26)

After another move, Priscilla and Aquila find themselves in the community of the faithful in Ephesus. Although Paul traveled with them from Corinth, he continued toward Jerusalem, as Priscilla and Aquila stayed in Ephesus. A new kid comes to the block by the name of Apollos. He is well trained and speaks quite well, but his knowledge is incomplete. However, Priscilla and Aquila see his potential, and know his heart is in the right place. Instead of calling him out in front of everyone and shaming him for presumptuously preaching an incomplete Gospel, they take him aside. They invite him into their counsel, rather than pushing him out of the community for not having his facts straight. They do not exclude him for his faulty preaching but teach him and by doing so, they bring him into the right belief.

Message Point 3: Bring People into Your Home (Romans 16:3–5)

Priscilla and Aquila move yet again, this time back to Rome where they had been before. There, they continue to invite people into the community of faith just as they have before. In Paul's letter to the Corinthian church, he mentions the church meeting in Priscilla and Aquila's home in Ephesus (1 Corinthians 16:19). From Paul's greeting, we also learn they host a church in their Roman home too (v. 5). Paul praises them for working together with him and even risking their lives for him. Even though this couple boasts only a few verses in the New Testament, Paul calls them "co-workers," seeing them as equals in the spread of Christianity. They have been the ones to invite people into their own homes—their own private, personal spaces—even if it required secrecy. This method of gathering as house-churches sustained the church through many years of persecution. Priscilla and Aquila's faithfulness to gathering house-churches brought people in, so that early Christians had a place to talk and worship together.

THAT'LL PREACH

I would be remiss to conclude a lesson about Priscilla and Aquila without highlighting the traveling they did. Aquila was from Pontus (Acts 18:2), the Roman province on the southern coast of the Black Sea, one of the farthest reaches of the Empire. Then, we see Priscilla and Aquila were in Rome (v. 2), the center of the Empire, over 1,000 miles from Pontus. Then in this text, they're in Corinth (v. 1), a major trading city. After that, they go with Paul to Ephesus on the other side of the Aegean Sea (vv. 18–19). Finally, in Romans, we glean that they are back in Rome (Romans 16:3). In Rome, in Corinth, and in Ephesus, they host the fledgling church. So we see that not only did they bring people in, but they also went out to the people.

CONCLUSION

Let us thank God for providing His Word and providing us examples in faith in that Word. He has let us see the amazing lives of Priscilla and Aquila as they went out and brought people in, into work, into the right belief, and into their own homes.

NOTES

_____

_____

_____

_____

_____

_____

_____

_____

_____

_____

_____

Lydia—An Unexpected Find

By CaReese Mukulu

Lesson Theme	Unit Theme	Scripture
Lydia: Called to Serve	The Call of Women	Acts 16:11–15, 40; 1 Corinthians 1:26–30

INTRODUCTION

Life is full of surprises. Paul, a church planter and apostle, was no exception to this. Paul's life was full of surprises, twists, and turns. However, Paul was faithful in His service to God even when things didn't go according to plan.

One example is found in Acts 16. In Troas, Paul had seen a vision of a man from Macedonia urging him to come and preach the Gospel there. When he arrived, however, Paul did not hesitate to minister to a group of women. As we will see, tremendous fruit will come from Paul's obedience.

MESSAGE POINTS

Message Point 1: An Unusual Situation (Acts 16:11–14)

Paul's pattern was to teach about Jesus at the local synagogue. This was most likely his plan for Philippi. Only he arrived to find that there was no synagogue. Scholars note that the city of Philippi must have had a limited Jewish population at that time otherwise; there would have been a synagogue. Ten Jewish males were required to establish a synagogue and these conditions were not met. Because there was no synagogue, Jews in Philippi met in other locations, like simple buildings, or even open-air settings for prayer. It was at such a gathering on the Gangites River, about 1.5 miles west of town, where Paul encountered Lydia.

Lydia was from Thyatira, a commercial city in Asia Minor. She was called a worshiper of God, indicating that she was not a proselyte of Judaism, but did worship with the Jews. Lydia was also a businesswoman; she sold purple cloth.

Paul shared the Gospel with the women he found in the city. The Scriptures are clear that God opened Lydia's heart to receive Paul's message. It was Paul's job to spread the Gospel, and he was faithful in his proclamation. God, however, illuminated the truth to Lydia.

Message Point 2: The Impact (v. 15)

The Scripture notes that Lydia and her household were baptized. This probably included her children and her servants. Lydia's hospitality suggests that she was a woman of considerable means. She was able to house Paul's missionary party of four in addition to her normal household.

The impact of Paul's ministry was that Lydia was saved. Her household was saved as well. Lydia then offered hospitality to Paul and his companions. Thereafter, the Philippian Christians met at Lydia's house.

Message Point 3: Seeing Things Differently (1 Corinthians 1:26–30)

In Paul's letter to the Corinthians, he reminds readers that God views things differently than people. God did not choose the Corinthians based on their wealth or status. He turned the world's convention on its head by choosing the ordinary.

This certainly went against the Corinthians' prideful tendencies. Wealth and status weren't God's criteria. God chose the things that many would disregard as a way to demonstrate His love and grace. God's salvation is based on grace, not our merit. This eliminates any opportunity for boasting. Rather, it gives everyone reason to celebrate the goodness and power of God.

THAT'LL PREACH

It is not uncommon for people to mistake the value of things, even commonplace things in the home. For example, lots of people throw out bananas once they develop broken spots. Many will regret not eating the bananas earlier; because once they are brown, people consider them unpalatable. In the eyes of an experienced baker, however, brown bananas are wonderful. An experienced baker will realize that brown bananas are ideal for baking banana bread. An experienced baker will take brown bananas to create something amazing where someone else would throw them away. The bananas are the same. The difference is that an experienced baker will recognize the value of the bananas where others would not.

In the same way, we may judge ministry opportunities by the wrong criteria. Our job is to be faithful to the things God has called us to. God has a way of making our obedience fruitful when we do.

CONCLUSION

Life has a way of surprising us. Ministry opportunities may not always be what we expect. The Book of Acts records Paul having a vision of a man from Macedonia, but when he arrives, he finds that this city doesn't even have a synagogue. Rather than preaching to a synagogue of Jewish men, he finds himself ministering to a small group of women by the water instead. Paul could have become frustrated because his expectations hadn't been met. Instead, he ministers faithfully to the women and the church at Philippi is born.

Like Paul, we may encounter situations where ministry opportunities don't match our expectations. God wants us to serve him faithfully wherever we find ourselves. What appears to be less than ideal by our criteria could have a tremendous impact by the Holy Spirit.

We see that as Paul was faithful in carrying out his mission Lydia was then able to carry out hers. She hosted the church in Philippi and became a faithful worker for the Gospel. Her family and the Philippian church were transformed by her faith.

NOTES

_____

_____

_____

_____

Armed With Information

By Daryl Hairston

Lesson Theme	Unit Theme	Scripture
Moses: Prophet of Deliverance	Faithful Prophets	Deuteronomy 18:15-22

INTRODUCTION

We live in a society where a barrage of words is constantly surrounding everyone. The collegiate dictionary is running at a fast pace with the use and misuse of words that flow from its pages. Everyone is trying to get words in the atmosphere without the thought that they might be negligent. The amazing chatter and utterance of words has brought about major competition. Everyone is pulling for their cause and pleading their case to the larger market, whether it's corporate America, schools, or religion. But one Word rises above the rest. God's Word has been spoken, tested, and tried for many years. God's words will always come to fruition. We must seek to take heed to God's words as we turn the page in the Bible. God's words are filled with information that can serve our concerns, care for our needs, comfort and grant peace. "You better mind what you say; you got to give an account at the judgment, you better mind."

MESSAGE POINTS

Message Point 1: An Honored Request (Deuteronomy 18:15–18)

The prophet Moses spoke of another prophet to follow him. That prophet would be armed with information that is clearly only from God. The prophet will be like Moses and will come from among his own people. Without exception, the prophet will speak the words of God. This demonstrates how God will raise up human instruments to be at His disposal. God has assignments for His creation, and He gives us the power from within to do His will. Still, we must be the ones to choose to do good. God will keep us in the process to carry out His prophetic words. We must be willing to trust God as human instruments, armed with information. That is not only appropriate for Israel but for generations to come.

Message Point 2: God Will Hold Us Accountable (vv. 19–20)

In today's society, the church has lessened God's word to fill pews, rather than transform lives. Distorting God's word will create a false perspective in the hearts and minds of people. It will cause the people to devalue the real prophets and give value to the false prophets. Remember: God's word has been tried, tested, and proven. God is going to hold those who are distorting God's word responsible. Church, let us not trade God's values for the valves of society to gain material values. The charlatans are out there. Many are leaving the church at an alarming rate, but this doesn't change the fact that God's word is true. We must read and study God's word for ourselves. James states, "We must not only be hearers of God's word, but doers." That is a true way to measure God's Word.

Message Point 3: Try God's Word For Yourself (vv. 21-22)

We must heed the voice of God. We must seek to measure and determine what we ask for. Will your blessing be a blessing to others? Is what you asked for clear and compelling to the heart? Did God grant the request? Now you have created a level of accountability. I know many voices are trying to gain entrance in our lives. Read God's Word for yourself. God's Word has been tried and tested. Yes, there will be prophets, who come along, who will not represent the true voice of God in order to gain something from you. If they are speaking false language, "they will die." We have a true God from whom we can gain so much understanding. It will benefit every facet of our lives. We must listen to the word of God that has been spoken by the prophets and measured by the time frame given by the prophet. God's presence was among the Israelites. God raised up Moses to continue speaking the words, and now God has raised up many for the proclamation of God's word. Hear ye the word of God.

THAT'LL PREACH

Many words are spoken with the hope that they will stick to people's heart. Many don't check the facts. They just dive in and believe. The act of believing without fact checking turns out many times to be devastating, because what many say might actually turn out misleading. Think about Jim Jones. His spoken words and use of words led many to their demise. On the other hand, God's word is true. Through the good times and bad times, God's words continues to rebuke falsehoods and transform, renew, forgive, and restore life. Open your hearts and offer yourself to God. Be willing to trust God. No one can deliver and make things happen like God. Let the word enter your hearts, so that you can experience the goodness and real truth of how promises can be fulfilled by trusting in God's Word.

CONCLUSION

God's Word is true, trusting, powerful, and real. Allow the mighty, powerful word of God to challenge you, as you trust and believe and see for yourself that God's word is real. "O taste and see that the LORD is good" (Psalm 34:8).

NOTES

_____

_____

_____

_____

_____

_____

_____

_____

_____

_____

We Can Take It!

By Dr. Joshua Mitchell

Lesson Theme	**Unit Theme**	**Scripture**
Joshua: Prophet of Conquest	Faithful Prophets	Joshua 5:13–6:5, 15–16, 20

INTRODUCTION

Have you ever been given a promise from God? Have you ever been given a promise from God that required some time and action on your part to take possession of? This is the reality for the people of Israel when we encounter Joshua and the people of Israel in our text. After a dramatic exit from Egypt and years of wandering in the wilderness, Joshua and the Israelites find themselves approaching the city of Jericho in the Promised Land of Canaan—a land inhabited by enemy opposition whose armies were no doubt prepared to defend the city. Through the narrative that unfolds in these verses, we learn some valuable lessons on how to take possession of all that God has promised us.

MESSAGE POINTS

Message Point 1: Heed Righteous Reminders (Joshua 5:13–15)

The people of Israel have finally made it to the edge of Canaan the Promised Land after years of wandering in the wilderness. As they approach the land, Joshua encounters a "man" standing between God's people and the Promised Land and their resulting conversation provides Joshua and the modern church with some reminders of God's role in the quest to take possession of God promises. The first reminder is that the resources of God accompany those who are actively on the Lord's side. When asked about who the man with the drawn sword is fighting for, Joshua learns that he commands the army of the Lord—but is "for" neither the Israelites nor their enemies. He does not pick a side. It reminds us that God does not play favorites based on what we call ourselves (in Israel's case, they see themselves as the people of God) but God will fight according to where we stand with God. Secondly, when Joshua is instructed to take off his shoes (v. 15), it is a re-enactment of what Moses experiences at the burning bush in Exodus 3. Joshua is being reminded through this ritual that as God was with Moses and the ancestors, God would also be with him. It is good news for the modern believer, to be reminded that the powerful God of the past is also the God who engages with us today.

Message Point 2: We Can Win Through Unconventional Undertakings (Joshua 6:1–5)

Once Joshua completes his encounter with the commander of the army of the Lord, God begins to speak to Joshua again. God assures Joshua that the city is ripe for the taking and grants him the assurance that God has already delivered them the victory over the armies at Jericho. Things get interesting, however, when God shares with Joshua how they would take the city. God does not instruct them to fight in the ways that military strategists would suggest. There is no mention of hand to hand combat, chariots, or bows and arrows. Instead, God provides a very unconventional strategy to get the victory: walk and shout! It is a reminder that when God is fighting with us, we do not have to fight as our enemies would, but God can grant victory through walks and shouts, stones and slingshots, and even through nails and crosses!

Message Point 3: Our Enemies Are Overtaken Through Obedience (vv. 15–20)

For some of the military men of Israel, I imagine that the idea of marching around the walls of the city for seven days may have seemed silly, even dangerous. Was it possible that Joshua heard God wrong? Despite the various thoughts and fears the people may have had about the unconventional undertaking God sent them on, verses 15–20 show that the people were *obedient*. They followed the command of the Lord, despite how unconventional it was, and as a result, the walls that fortified their enemies and stood as a boundary between them and promised territory crumpled. Through obedience to God, despite unconventional methods, they were able to take the city. It is a lesson to modern believers that sometimes the only barrier to taking possession of what God plans to provide for us is our own willingness to be obedient to God's instructions.

THAT'LL PREACH

As a child, I didn't have access to the same technology that young children have access to today. To be entertained, we played all kinds of games outside—kickball, tag, capture the flag, dodgeball, and my personal favorite—"Simon Says." On its surface, "Simon Says" was not a difficult game. To win, all a player had to do was listen and perform the actions that the leader, Simon, would say. I observed that my friends would not win the game because instead of focusing and listening to what Simon *said* to do, they were caught up on watching and trying to figure out what Simon was *doing* while we played. In the game of life, we don't take our cues from Simon but from God. And if we will commit to listening and doing what God *says*, instead of being tripped up on what we think God is *doing*, we will find that we will stand victoriously in short order!

CONCLUSION

We are often excited about the promises God makes to us, yet God's promises sometimes come with opposition and the need for action on our parts. We must remember that the same God who provided resources for our ancestors is also with us when we are in alignment with God. God may require some unconventional undertakings to gain possession of the promises, but if we are obedient—we can take it!

NOTES

_____

_____

_____

_____

_____

_____

_____

_____

_____

The Unsung Hero

By Dr. Matthew C. Jones

Lesson Theme	Unit Theme	Scripture
Huldah: Prophet of Wisdom	Faithful Prophets	2 Kings 22:14–20

INTRODUCTION

The world-renown poet and civil rights activist, Maya Angelou, once said, "How important it is for us to recognize and celebrate our heroes and she-roes." In 2 Kings 22, we read of such a she-ro and a couple of heroes in the mix as well. In fact, the chapter begins with a hero named Josiah, who as a young boy became king of Judah. During his ascent into leadership, Josiah stood up against the forces of darkness and sought to lead the Jewish people into God's will (see 2 Kings 22–23, and 2 Chronicles 34–35). He led a reform to renovate the Temple of God in Jerusalem and called the struggling nation to repentance. In the midst of this movement, an unsung she-ro named Huldah arose. We meet her in the text of 2 Kings 22:8–20 (cf. 2 Chronicles 34:22–28), in which this unassuming heroine emerges to faithfully serve God in a desperate hour of great need.

MESSAGE POINTS

Message Point 1: Huldah the Prophetess (2 Kings 22:14)

In 2 Kings 22:14, we read Huldah was a prophetess contemporary with Jeremiah and Zephaniah. Like her collaborators, she was a powerful mouthpiece for the Lord at this critical time. Being a prophetess is not a title one gives to herself: rather, it is a specific position given by God alone to a special selected few of His children. The people of promise were unraveling ethically and spiritually, with a long series of morally bankrupt kings. With Josiah as the king, there was hope of a new day. Unfortunately, none of the kings after him followed God's law as faithfully. This was a sobering reality for the prophetic ministry of Huldah, namely, she would minister in a rather short-lived moment of spiritual renewal. In verse 14 of 2 Kings 22, we see the leaders of the people came to her for direction from the Lord to discern the times and seek God's will.

Message Point 2: Heroes and Providence (vv. 15–18)

In the providence of God, Huldah was positioned to point her people to the law of God and His covenantal faithfulness to His promises. In the wilderness coming to their new homeland, the Mosaic covenant was given to the people which promised both blessings for obedience and curses for disobedience to the law of God (Exodus 19–24, Deuteronomy 28). Huldah called the people to see the ramifications to their sin conditioned under the Law of Moses. Meanwhile, she also held fast to the unconditional guarantees of God to Abraham and David, in the trust of the Lord's providence. As a prophetess, God communicated through her that judgment was coming, calling the people to humble penitence in the sovereign promises of the Lord of the covenants.

Message Point 3: Humbled and Penitent (vv. 19–20)

According to 2 Kings 22:19, the revelation of the prophetess Huldah extended mercy to Josiah, in light of his contrite heart before God. In the Bible we read that this experience of the heart in embracing repentance and faith are wondrous gifts from the Savior brought to sinners by his grace (Acts 11:18; 2 Timothy 2:25; Ephesians 2:8). The fruit of these gifts are displayed in transformed living that gives birth to good works (James 2:14–18; Matthew 7:16–20). In the case of Josiah, the prophetess revealed the just judgment of God would not fall on his head and instead he would go on to bring reform to Israel (2 Kings 23:1–14) and die before the coming of judgment on Israel. In fact, Josiah passed about four years before Babylon's first attack on Jerusalem, which was about 605 years before Jesus.

THAT'LL PREACH

The first half of 2 Kings traces the history of the divided kingdom of Israel in gross dysfunction and darkness. Penetrating the night comes our she-ro Huldah, the prophetess, offering words of prophecy and hope about God's faithfulness, with allusions to a bigger unfolding divine story. While 2 Kings records the death of Josiah and his burial, prophetic history testifies that his descendant—our Lord Jesus—could not be held in the grave (2 Timothy 2:8). Further, while the reign of Josiah lasted a little over 30 years, the coming Kingdom of Jesus will last forever. As noted in this message, our King died for His people and in the promises of God, He will fulfill every dimension of the covenants in Scripture and defeat all of the enemies of His people, including sin and death itself. Babylonia may have won in the days following Josiah, but we read in Revelation 18:2 that, "Babylon the great is fallen, is fallen." According to prophecy, King Jesus will come (Revelation 19), establish the Davidic throne (Revelation 20) and He will usher in a new heaven and earth (Revelation 21). In the gospel of Matthew, both the victory of Babylonia and Josiah are mentioned in the historical genealogy of Jesus (Matthew 1:12, 17). It is clear from this and the storyline of the Bible that the greatest hero of all is none other than our risen Lord, Jesus.

CONCLUSION

In 2 Kings 22, we meet a great she-ro of faith, who inspires our souls by her ostensibly unsung work as a prophetess. The author shows her in high esteem, but the people in the story do not seem to value Huldah's voice. Like the quoted poet Maya Angelou, she very likely had to overcome discrimination, prejudice, and abuse in her lifetime. Huldah spoke for her people and goes down in history as a great prophetesses, next to other prophetic she-ro figures such as Miriam (Exodus 15:20), Deborah (Judges 4:4), the wife of Isaiah (Isaiah 8:3), Anna (Luke 2:36), and the four daughters of Philip the evangelist (Acts 21:8–9). These prophetesses of Scripture served God faithfully in their lives and one day we will meet them in the Kingdom of Lord in the resurrection that is come. May the Lord make us and find us faithful—as he did Huldah—in this generation. Amen.

NOTES

_____

_____

_____

_____

_____

_____

In-Courage

By John Burton, Jr.

Lesson Theme	Unit Theme	Scripture
Elijah: Prophet of Courage	Faithful Prophets	1 Kings 18:5-18

INTRODUCTION

What does courage look like? Many times, people believe it looks like a police officer, firefighter, or soldier serving in the military. While others think it's the person who stands up for the underdog, the downtrodden, or the forgotten. Courage does not always look as some believe it should. Obadiah's life did not look very courageous. If anything, it personified fear. After a chance encounter with his fellow believer, the prophet Elijah, his feelings of personal inadequacies would surface. This reality seems inconceivable when at one time he exuded a multitude of courage by hiding 100 prophets from Jezebel's massacre. Now he is shrouded with timidity at the simplest request from Elijah to tell the king of his whereabouts. So a life once seasoned with proactivity and progress is now peppered with doubt and fear. However, what looks like a story of coincidence transposes into a chronicle of God's providence.

MESSAGE POINTS

Message Point 1: The Invitation (1 Kings 18:7–8)

After a period of dodging King Ahab, God's call to Elijah is to present himself. But how? It's a chance encounter with his brother in the faith, Obadiah, that provides the opportunity. Elijah invites Obadiah to be a participant in the divine encounter. Who better to ask than Obadiah, who is in the king's employ and has favor with him? He doesn't have to do any spectacular feat or slay hundreds of people. All Elijah asks of him is to alert King Ahab of his presence. What an easy task and a privilege! Just like Elijah and Obadiah, God wants us to participate in His divine work on earth. Regularly God asks that we join Him in work He is embarking in. It may not be a gigantic task, like saving someone from a burning building. It can be as minuscule as saying hello, offering someone in need a dollar, or hugging someone. As the body of Christ, we are to be His functionality in the world (1 Corinthians 12:27). If He asks, He will always provide the resources to get the task completed. Notice Elijah asked Obadiah while he was already on an assignment for King Ahab. God invitations and tasks can occur at any moment. We just have to be open and available to heed His request.

Message Point 2: The Rationalization (vv. 9–14)

When God told Elijah to go, he went. However, Obadiah reacts differently. He bursts into a litany of reasons he is unable to perform the act while the truth is, he is not willing to. Obadiah has become a victim of disorganized thinking. He is paralyzed by his fear. It wasn't a fright of the surety but the anxiety of the unknown. He believed Ahab would kill him. He assumed that Elijah would flee. Obadiah looked for rationalization to say no, not only to Elijah but essentially to God. Often times we want to be used greatly by God. Silently we say, "Here am I; send me" (Isaiah 6:8). When God takes us up on the offer, we soon provide a plethora of excuses on why we can't fulfill the assignment. We cannot allow fear to render us immobile when it comes to serving God. He has gifted us with three powerful resources: power, love, and a sound mind to utilize (2 Timothy 1:7). It's not a matter of what is true but a matter of what we think. Therefore, we have to constantly capture our rebellious thoughts and make it obedient to Christ (2 Corinthians 10:5). We have a unique contrast: Elijah, who accepts his assignment without question, and Obadiah, who questioned making a simple announcement. Which one are you?

Message Point 3: The Motivation (vv. 15–18)

Everyone needs a word of encouragement. Obadiah was no different. Elijah knew he had to aid in calming and encouraging his friend. He declared, "As the LORD of hosts liveth" (v. 15). Elijah swears not by any power or special privilege of his own but by the strength and sovereignty of God. In doing so, he alerts Obadiah that he too was standing and walking in faith with the Almighty God. Not being truthful to his commitment to him would not only discredit Elijah's right standing as a good witness for God. He assured Obadiah saying, "I will surely shew myself unto him to day" (v. 15). Elijah's commitment to Obadiah was sealed with a time and date stamp with one word "today." It was with this assurance that Obadiah was motivated to action without another word. Equally, Elijah was probably encouraged himself in the Lord (1 Samuel 30:6). Once he uttered those words to Obadiah, there was no turning back for him either. Obadiah, and more importantly God, was relying on him to fulfill his commitment to the task at hand. Therefore, when the overdue encounter with King Ahab arrived, he was confident. This is evidenced by immediately taking the conversation to Ahab's disobedience to God.

THAT'LL PREACH

One of my favorite childhood movies is *The Wizard of Oz*. Rounding out the foursome of Dorothy, the Scarecrow, and the Tin Man is the Lion. He was not just any lion, his full name was the Cowardly Lion. This is a weird juxtaposition because lions are supposed to be the king of all beasts. He felt his fear rendered him inadequate to face life's challenges. So he often retreated in the times of danger and fright. The lion deems his life unbearable because he lacks courage. Consequently, he invites himself into Dorothy's company to see the Wizard to receive some. Once the lion meets the Wizard and receives a medal of courage he feelsconfident. Although the medal had no power, Lion believed it did. Like Dorothy's desire to go home, he possessed the power the entire time. It was not the medal but merely adjusting his mindset. Jesus' Cross is just a symbol but believing in what the Cross symbolizes means we can walk in victory. It serves as a source of encouragement.

CONCLUSION

Courage can come in many forms. To be honest, courage looks like you and me. It's not when we do enormous heroic acts, but when we simply stand up in the ordinary. Courage doesn't wear a uniform, a cape, or even a medal; it's dressed in plain clothes. Because it's not about the form or fashion but all about the faith. It's totally trusting yourself to do what's right with the confidence that God is with you. Be "in-couraged"!

NOTES

_____

_____

_____

_____

_____

_____

We are Saved By The Blood of the Lamb

By Dr. Michael K. Roussell

Lesson Theme	**Unit Theme**	**Scripture**
Salvation is Sealed	Prophets of Restoration	Luke 24:13–16, 22–35

INTRODUCTION

Living standards in today's world have never been higher since the Garden of Eden. Our generation has conveniences, comforts, labor-saving devices, and recreational facilities of which no previous generation has ever dreamed. And still, the strain of living continues to weigh down on us in this day of struggles, anxieties, tensions, and the tribulations of this world. In the book of John, the 16th chapter, the Lord spoke concerning the trials and tribulations of this world. He said, "These things I have spoken unto you, that in me ye might have peace. In the world ye shall have tribulation: but be of good cheer; I have overcome the world" (John 16:33). The unbeliever looking with sin-dimmed eyes at a poorly lighted world might well despair. However, the believer, instructed in the Word of God and illumined by the Holy Spirit, should be able to read what comes and still yet experience joyful days with restful nights. For we know that after His suffering, He rose; and through His suffering, we are saved.

MESSAGE POINTS

Message Point 1: He Died On The Cross For Our Sins (Luke 24:26)

Christ's death on the Cross is the sacrifice that atones for our sins (1 John 2:2). Since sin has separated us from God (Isaiah 59:2), Jesus died to take away our sin so that we would no longer experience that separation. The punishment for our sin is death. But Jesus, God's only begotten Son, died on the Cross. He paid the penalty for our sins so that we might have an eternal relationship with Him (John 3:16). Far from being the kind of God who would keep Himself separate from His creation, Jesus is willing to pay any price to be with us. He even tells His disciples on the road to Emmaus that the Messiah must suffer (Luke 24:26). Thank God He did! Because of His sacrifice: (1) Thou shalt be saved, (2) Thou shalt be delivered, (3) Thou shalt be healed, (4) Thou shalt be set free, (5) Thou shalt have peace, (6) Thou shalt have joy, and (7) Your life shall be changed. In Jesus' Name!

Message Point 2: Jesus Rose Up From The Dead (vv. 16, 30–33)

In Luke 24, Cleopas and another encounter the resurrected Jesus while the way to Emmaus. Initially, they were unable to recognize Him (v. 16). However, when Jesus supped with them, He revealed Himself to them. After Jesus vanished, Cleophas and the other went back to Jerusalem to tell the disciples that Jesus had risen (vv. 30-33).

Now that He is risen and we accept Jesus as the Lord and Savior of our lives, He begins to: (1) Restore our consciousness, (2) Restore a Godly Spirit, (3) Impart new health to us, (4) Renew our minds, (5) Restore vitality, (6) Restore effectiveness, and (7) Restore our currency. He begins to put us back in operative condition. We will then be able and ready to walk upright before God and man. He is well able and worthy to be praised!

Message Point 3: Jesus Is Coming Again (v. 34)

Jesus is alive! What excitement we can share with His disciples to report, "The Lord is risen indeed!" (v. 34). He is living in the world today. Many witnesses saw Him and spoke with Him after His resurrection. Furthermore, we do know that He is coming back again. Matthew tells us, we "shall see the Son of man coming in the clouds of heaven with power and great glory" (Matthew 24:30). Luke continues that Jesus "shall so come in manner as ye have seen him go into heaven" (Acts 1:11). He is coming back for a church without spot or wrinkle; holy, without blemish (Ephesians 5:7). It is time for us to get ready because He is coming back again!

THAT'LL PREACH

It is the Carpenter from Nazareth that still repairs broken hearts. It is Jesus that still restores broken homes. It is the Carpenter from Nazareth that still repairs fractured dreams and shattered relationships. It is of the Lord's mercies that we are not consumed. Great is His faithfulness! Jesus died on the Cross. It is finished. For those who believe, when we all get to heaven, there will be no more dying there, no more sickness and no more pain. It is finished. Thank You, Lord!

CONCLUSION

The recorded history states that after the Resurrection of our Lord, His status changed. His Glory was revealed, His goodness displayed, and He had all power intact. Because He is alive, He defeated Satan, He provided victory, and our hope is in Him. The songwriter wrote, "My hope is built on nothing less than Jesus' blood and righteousness, … on Christ the Solid Rock I stand." Our faith in that rock is immovable because of the resurrection.

NOTES

_____

_____

_____

_____

_____

_____

_____

_____

_____

_____

_____

_____

Do the Right Thing

By R. Neal Siler

Lesson Theme	Unit Theme	Scripture
Ezra: Faith and Action Preacher	Prophets of Restoration	Ezra 10:1-12

INTRODUCTION

They were worshipping in the restored Temple. It should have been a time of great joy and satisfaction. Ezra was upset at the news that all was not well. In fact, he was hurt to the point of tears. He had been ministering to the spiritual needs of the people when he learns that all is not well. He discovers that despite God's great goodness, many of them have deliberately disobeyed God's command. It shouldn't have been a hard thing to do. Doing the right thing should have been a natural response to God's goodness.

MESSAGE POINTS

Message Point 1: It's hard to do the right thing when you make rules for your behavior (Ezra 10:1–2)

One of the most powerful and loving things you can do for yourself and your world is to do what is right. There is no mystery in this. God has told you what is right, and Jesus has demonstrated it. But in our "do what you want," "whatever feels good" world, God's message has gotten lost. We are told to do what we feel deep down is the right thing for us. There are no universal absolutes. Everything is relative, so we make rules for our behavior and we define our standard of right. But this ultimately grieves the heart of God and breaks our hearts in the process.

What is the right thing? When the congregation saw the pain of their disobedience in the countenance of their priest they cried, "We have trespassed against our God, and have taken strange wives of the people of the land" (from v. 2). In other words, "We knew better, God told us what was right. The right thing was faithful obedience to God's rule, but we made our own rules."

Message Point 2: When you play by God's rules, you always win (v. 6)

It broke Ezra's heart, but he had enough faith to believe God for the people. He went into prayer and deep intercession for their sin, and it got results. There is a lesson in that methodology for us. Maybe sometimes instead of trying to convince people how they should live, we ought to let them know our heart is broken, as God's heart is broken, because we want so much for them to get what God has to offer. Maybe if we pray and intercede instead of fuss and argue, God will move on their heart. God's rules always allow for us to return. Not even our disobedience is powerful enough to destroy hope when we return to Him. He has made provision for us to re-enter His covenant. All it requires is a confession and a commitment. A confession: I have done wrong. A commitment: I want to do better. What is so amazing is that although Ezra lamented discovering the wickedness of the faithful during a time of thanksgiving, hope was not lost.

Message Point 3: When You Change the Rules, You Change the Game (vv. 11–12)

The game changes when you change the rules. When you live by your rules, individual behaviors become precedents for new rules. This only digs a deeper ditch that creates unfulfilled longings, wounds, and brokenness. Why? Because your rules are not in concert with God's desires, and when your desires are in conflict with God's, you see more of yourself than you see of God. When you get in the way of yourself, even though God sees you, you experience emptiness. You get stuck in negative thought loops. Then because you let yourself down, you don't believe you are capable of doing the right thing. Your negative belief holds you in this game of defeat. Change the rule and it will change the game.

Ezra came before the people. He tells them, God's rule says, "Now therefore make confession unto the LORD God of your fathers, and do his pleasure: and separate yourselves from the people of the land, and from the strange wives" (v. 11). When they heard this, I am sure there were moments of reflection and conflict. I am sure there were those in the group who loved the game as it was, but they were smart enough to know this. The rules we've made for our behavior cannot bring us the promises of God. So, the whole assembly changed the rule, as we read: "Then all the congregation answered and said with a loud voice, As thou hast said, so must we do" (v. 12).

THAT'LL PREACH

Somebody said, "Character is doing the right thing when nobody's looking. There are too many people who think that the only thing that's right is to get by, and the only thing that's wrong is to get caught." As faulty as this logic may be, resident in this thinking is the beauty of God's hope— His hope that we will get it. Expect to mess up and do the wrong thing sometimes. That's okay. Hope gives us confidence that no context or situation's unfavorable to our survival, because hope is the conviction that God has it all in control. But when you realize you have missed it, cry like Ezra. Weep like Jeremiah. Repent like the people of the congregation and allow the flood of God's love to break the rules, change the game, and fill you with hope.

CONCLUSION

If we are not careful, we can engage in distorted informational processing to avoid our guilt. But this only keeps us in bondage to our own rules. In our bondage we will not get it—that our only hope is in God. That hope comes as we acknowledge our condition, humble ourselves, pray, seek God's face, and turn from our wicked ways. Only then God says He will hear from Heaven and will forgive our sin and heal our land (Jeremiah 29:12–13). Doing the right thing is always the right thing. It feels good, it's the right thing to do, it brings you closer to others and closer to God. It will transform your life.

NOTES

_____

_____

_____

_____

_____

_____

Strategic Planning

By Rev. Michael Easley

Lesson Theme	Unit Theme	Scripture
Nehemiah: The Captive Cupbearer Rebuilds a Nation	Prophets of Restoration	Nehemiah 2:11-20

INTRODUCTION

God is calling us to be spiritual leaders. Whether it is in our home, church, workplace, or anywhere else, we are called to lead our lives in such a way that others want to follow. As leaders, we are called to be strategic planners, with God as our focus. Our passage today relays the story of Nehemiah and his leadership. Through his example, we can learn how to be God-centered, prepared leaders.

MESSAGE POINTS

Message Point 1: The Survey (Nehemiah 2:11–16)

Upon arrival, Nehemiah did not rush into action but rested for three days. Then, he covertly inspected the situation. Nehemiah said in these verses that he did not disclose his plans to anyone, not to the enemies nor his fellow workers until he had accurate information. His route is traced in these verses. If seen on a map, this trek proved to be a thorough assessment of the city's condition. How often do we as Christians run blindly into ministry, as if it is random or mindless! Jesus, when speaking about following him, said, "Or what king, going to make war against another king, sitteth not down first, and consulteth whether he be able with ten thousand to meet him that cometh against him with twenty thousand?" (Luke 14:31). We are to be "wise as serpents, and harmless as doves" (Matthew 10:16).

Message Point 2: The Report (vv. 17–18)

Nehemiah exposed the negative situation: the land was desolate and the gates were burned. Then he reported the positive, "I told them of the hand of my God which was good upon me; as also the king's words that he had spoken unto me" (from v. 18). After the reminder of God's goodness, the people responded positively. Do we as God's people get discouraged too easily? We're to focus on God's promises and believe.

Message Point 3: The Opposition (vv. 19–20)

Now a third enemy entered the picture, Geshem. Some scholars feel he was the most powerful of all the opponents. He and his son ruled a confederacy of Arabian tribes that were in control of Moab and Edom. Surrounded with opposition, Nehemiah's answer was, "The God of heaven, he will prosper us; therefore we his servants will arise and build" (v. 20). Notice he did not say, "King Artaxerxes will wipe you out if you mess with us!" No, his faith was in the God of heaven! He continued, telling them, "ye have no portion, nor right, nor memorial, in Jerusalem" (v. 20). Imagine, Jerusalem was in rubble and yet he boasted that the Lord would fulfill His promise!

How often do you watch or read the news and hear a story that just makes you wonder, "Who's in charge here? Someone actually approved that? Someone made a plan and that was it?" After hearing stories like that you might come up with how you would have done it much differently, much better, with just a few obvious adjustments. What do you do after you make that plan, though? Do you just sit back and watch the system continue in its dysfunction? Do you feel smug in the feeling that you know so much better? Or do you actually offer to help? Nehemiah saw a problem that truly disturbed him. It was a big problem that required lots of executive skills to fix, and those were just the skills Nehemiah had. He did not choose to sit back and hope the situation would fix itself, or hope that someone else would fix it. No, God raised him up to be a leader who would figure out how to solve the problem and guide people to accomplish the goal.

CONCLUSION

It's been said that God never gives His people tasks they can fulfill on their own. We will find ourselves in positions to glorify the Lord in such incredible ways that we don't believe they are possible. However, these are the very plans the Lord has for us. We will encounter hostility, we will have to survey and plan, and we will have to persuade others to continue in faith. If we, like Nehemiah, have an unshakable faith and commitment to God's promises, we will see incredible fulfillment, not only rebuilding a wall or a city but also bringing nations to faith in Jesus Christ!

NOTES

_____

_____

_____

_____

_____

_____

_____

_____

_____

_____

_____

_____

_____

_____

Hoping Against Hope

By Pastor Tommy E. Smith, Jr.

Lesson Theme	Unit Theme	Scripture
A Plea for Restoration	Prophets of Restoration	Lamentations 5

INTRODUCTION

Of all the ministerial assignments given to the servants of God, Jeremiah's has to rank as one of the most difficult. This servant of God had the thankless task of warning the nation during its last two decades of existence that if they did not change their ways, they would be no more. Unfortunately, his message was not heeded, and he painfully witnessed Judah's overthrow by Babylonia. As if watching this completely avoidable defeat wasn't enough, Jeremiah followed this up by trying to express the deep emotional turmoil this caused. This sorrowful anguish is the subject of the book of Lamentations (generally thought to have been written by Jeremiah). It is a rare literary occurrence for a book to be so beautifully written (it is an acrostic poem) to describe such devastating events, yet this too reflects something of God—His ability to reveal beauty in even the most dire conditions. In this last chapter of the book, Jeremiah makes a final effort on behalf of the nation to fully acknowledge their responsibility for this calamity and their total dependence on God's grace for restoration.

MESSAGE POINTS

Message Point 1: A Desperate Plea for Compassion (Lamentations 5:1–6)

On behalf of his beloved nation, Jeremiah opens this chapter with an impassioned plea for God's mercy and compassion as He considers Judah's plight. He reminds God that these are His people, specially chosen by Him to represent His truths to the rest of the nations. But instead of demonstrating the inherent advantages of being closely aligned with God, there is only a litany of failure, loss, and devastation. Their inheritance is ruined, their families shattered, their economy completely upended. They are subjected to the indignity of forced labor and can find no rest from their ceaseless persecutions. Jeremiah even points out that they have had to appeal to two former enemies, the Egyptians and Assyrians, to get enough bread for subsistence. Having previously made note of God's tremendous faithfulness (Lamentations 3:22–23), he can only hope that God's commitment to His covenant people will once again cause Him to be moved with compassion on their behalf.

Message Point 2: Acknowledging Sin and Accepting Responsibility (vv. 7–16)

Throughout this lament, Jeremiah is conscientious about not misplacing the blame for their predicament. In these verses, he is frank about admitting that this calamity is the result of their sustained sinfulness, and they were duly warned about this outcome. Acknowledging their role in creating this predicament is a noble stance to take, but that is not sufficient to release them from the outcome and the suffering their actions have produced. Errors in judgment will continue to plague our lives, and like Jeremiah, the nobler among us will approach God honestly and admit our wrongs. God has promised to grant forgiveness, but having a clean slate of forgiveness does not necessarily release us from the consequences of our sin. This is the difficult truth Judah had to live with. They were subjected to every form of social indignity, poverty, and violation of human decency, and so devastated that their hearts had nearly fainted from hopelessness.

Message Point 3: No Other Help (vv. 19–22)

In the final analysis, there is but one course of action left for Judah: an unrestrained appeal to God's mercy. Judah's calamities at this time were the worst it had ever faced. They can mount no defense. They can offer no resistance. The punishment has been carried out by the hand of a foreign power, and their disposition toward Israel was not likely to change anytime soon. But as powerful as Babylon was, they did not have the last word. Jeremiah here notes that, in the final analysis, God is the sovereign of the universe. He lives and rules forever, and He alone has the last word! His people know He can deliver, and they know He wants to teach them a lesson. Their question is, "Lord, how long?" "Have you forgotten us?" "What is the delay?" They know God is capable of giving them a complete turnaround—physically and spiritually. Their cautious question is, "Will He?" It almost seems like He has rejected them, but they are hoping against hope that God's love will prevail.

THAT'LL PREACH

Learning your lesson and paying your debt are generally agreed to be two conditions that must be met before any kind of absolution from judgment is granted. However, while these are necessary, they do not guarantee someone's release from the long-term consequences of their sin. Judah knew this and hoped against hope that God's mercy would give them the release they sought. Obtaining deliverance through a final, last-ditch appeal is not simply a foreign concept of a bygone era. It is actually something we have enshrined into law in this country. The governors of most states, and the President himself, have the power to grant clemency or pardons for offenses committed under their jurisdictions. There have been cases where inmates have exhausted every legal remedy available to no avail, leaving them with no other option than to serve out their sentence. Imagine the sheer joy of a prisoner facing a life sentence suddenly being set free by a governor's gracious act of clemency! This is what Jeremiah was praying for. More to the point, this is what all who believe were granted by Jesus as a result of His death and resurrection—an early release from an eternal sentence!

CONCLUSION

There are some cases where, after a fall, a person can work their way back up to where they were previously. There are also many cases where, once fallen, being restored is a decision that can only be made by someone other than the offender. Jeremiah knew that Judah's sin was such that they had fully earned the punishment they were enduring and could only rely on God's mercy for restoration. This is the state of affairs for all humanity. Our fall from God's grace is not something we can recover from or atone for. Only God's sovereign decision can deliver us from the duly earned sentence. Wondrously, salvation through Jesus does more than restore us. Christ places us far above where we started and allows us to share eternity as a member of His family!

NOTES

_____

_____

_____

_____

Mark My Words

By R. Neal Siler

Lesson Theme	Unit Theme	Scripture
Micaiah: Speaking Truth to Power	Courageous Prophets of Change	1 Kings 22:15-23, 26-28

INTRODUCTION

In 1 Kings 22:28 Micaiah declares, "Everyone mark my words!" (NLT). At some point or another, you have probably heard this phrase. Such an imprecation implies with great conviction that what is being said is true. Time will bear it out and the moment is to be noted for later verification that it happened just like they said it would!

"Mark my words, she will regret this when it all comes to light."
"Mark my words, he will be sorry he didn't listen to the whole story."
"Mark my words, if you aren't careful, everybody is going to leave you."
"Mark my words, that rascal is no good for you."

In other words, I have history and experience with situations like these, so pay attention, heed what I am saying, or you will pay the consequences! The phrase, "mark my words" was first used by Miles Coverdale in 1535 in his translation of the Bible in the book of Isaiah. Whenever it was used, it almost always suggested something bad was about to happen because someone refused to heed the warning. Such is the case in our text today.

MESSAGE POINTS

Message Point 1: Be Certain It's the Right Motive (1 Kings 22:1–5)

When you are called upon to speak truth to power, if you go about it the wrong way or if your motives are not right, you can hurt people. Our text opens with Ahab and Jehoshaphat together. There was a city that Ahab hoped to take, but he needed the help of Jehoshaphat if the battle was to be won. The King of Israel said to his officials, "Know ye that Ramoth in Gilead is ours, and we be still, and take it not out of the hand of the king of Syria?" (v. 3) He asked Jehoshaphat, "Wilt thou go with me to battle to Ramothgilead?" (v. 4) Jehoshaphat replied, "I am as thou art, my people as thy people, my horses as thy horses" (v. 5). But Jehoshaphat also said to the King of Israel, "Enquire, I pray thee, at the word of the LORD to day" (1 Kings 22:5). Jehoshaphat knew who he was dealing with and the possibility of trickery or deception was great. He had long since learned not everyone who says they are with you is necessarily with you or at best they are not "in it" for the same reasons you are. So before you do anything, enter any enterprise, seek the right counsel and make sure you have the right motives.

Message Point 2: Be Clear It's the Right Messenger (vv. 6–28)

Don't seek counsel from just anybody, though. Seek the right messenger who will speak what the Lord has said, not what the people want to hear. The right messenger will help you if you will listen. When Ahab asked his prophets, "Shall I go against Ramothgilead to battle?" they answered, "Go" (v. 6). That is what he wanted to hear. But Jehoshaphat quickly recognized these are not prophets of the true God and he asks, "Is there not here a prophet of the LORD besides, that we might enquire of him?" (v. 7). Enter Micaiah! They try to persuade Micaiah to agree with the false prophets. But Micaiah is clear, "As the LORD liveth, what the LORD saith unto me, that will I speak" (v. 14). Micaiah says to Ahab, "Now therefore, behold, the LORD hath put a lying spirit in the mouth of all these thy prophets, and the LORD hath spoken evil concerning thee" (v. 23). Ahab, who doesn't like this message, says, "Put this fellow in the prison, and feed him with bread of affliction and with water of affliction, until I come in peace" (v. 27). Micaiah declared, "If thou return at all in peace, the LORD hath not spoken by me." Then he added, "Everyone mark my words!" (v. 28, NLT). It will cost you dearly if you ignore the counsel of God's messenger.

Message Point 3: Be Confident It's the Right Message (v. 29)

When it is God's messenger, you can be confident it's also the right message. Jehoshaphat didn't listen (v. 29). So Ahab, king of Israel, and Jehoshaphat, king of Judah, went up to Ramoth Gilead. But as the story ends, the battle was not in their favor. It was just as Micaiah had said. During the battle, a single arrow struck him between the sections of his armor and Ahab bled to death. The word of the Lord that Micaiah spoke came true. Not listening to the right message cost Ahab his life and Jehoshaphat his integrity.

THAT'LL PREACH

In, "The Valley of Hope: A Fable About Self-Discovery and Destiny," Carolyn Landsman tells the story of Ping, the smooth baby ball born to the Pong family who thought he was destined to be a great golf ball. No matter what, he never measured up. Echoing in his mind were the words of his friends, family, and coaches, "Who do you think you are? You will never amount to anything? You are not good enough. Loser! You don't have what it takes. Mark my words, you'll amount to nothing." In despair he runs away. He meets the great Ping Fu, who tells him: "Ping, your problem is in whom you have been listening to. You are round and smooth like a golf ball. Everyone expected you to be a golf ball, and you have tried to live a golf ball life. But if you will peel back the layers, you will find you are not a golf ball at all. Golf balls are hard inside and out. You are delicate on the outside and soft on the inside which allows you to float on water. A golf ball sinks in water. Being a golf ball was never your destiny." With that, he introduced Ping to the game of ping pong. Moving from side to side of the table with artful ease Ping realized how effortless it was for him to be who he really was—not a champion at the game of golf, but a champion of the game of ping pong. All his life he had been listening to the wrong words.

CONCLUSION

Whose words are you listening to? It's so easy to cave to the loudest voice with the greatest claims of happiness and success. These voices are often self-serving, and if we are not careful, we can be duped by their eloquence. We then fall into the trap of thinking that we can do whatever we want, that our pleasure and happiness is the only thing that matters. We get caught up in the entitlement trap and will not listen to the words that hold the message of life—the promise of love and fulfillment that can only come from God. Mark my words. If we listen to the wrong messenger, buy the wrong message, and are guided by the wrong motives, the fallout can be deadly—literally!

NOTES

_____

_____

_____

_____

Your Hand Has Been Swapped!

By Ramon Mayo

Lesson Theme	Unit Theme	Scripture
Isaiah: Offering Hope for the Future	Courageous Prophets of Change	Isaiah 29:13–24

INTRODUCTION

I love playing board games and card games. One of my favorites is the card game UNO. What I really love is how you may think things are going your way but then someone has a card that changes everything. It could be the reverse card or the wild card or the draw four card. You may think you're on the verge of winning or on the edge of losing, but one card can change it all. One of the things they've added is a card that makes you switch out your hand with another player. You could be just about ready to call UNO but if someone puts down the swap hands card, then they get your hand and you could get a hand with 14 cards of the same color. Everything that's been happening in the game and that you thought was going to happen is now reversed. And this is the way life in the kingdom works.

Isaiah 29:13–24 gives us a prophetic picture of how the kingdom of God reverses the situations of different types of people and turns our world upside down. And so we are going to look at Isaiah's picture of kingdom reversal and how your hand in life can be swapped!

MESSAGE POINTS

Message Point 1: The ways of hypocrites will be swapped (Isaiah 29:13–16)

Isaiah begins this prophecy by calling out hypocritical worship. He says the people of Judah have an outward appearance of worshiping God but their hearts are far from Him. They appear to know God but they really don't. God is going to reverse their position. The people who think they are wise and getting away with things while acting pious will be judged.

The outward appearance they are putting on will not be of any help because God's judgments will show who they really are. This is a warning and a call for you to be sincere and genuine in your worship and devotion to God. It will mean nothing for you to have lips that sing the best worship songs if the worship does not reach your heart.

Message Point 2: The injustice of oppressors will be swapped (vv. 17–21)

Isaiah delivers good news to those who are oppressed. God is coming to reign! The deaf will hear. The poor will be rich. The humble will be exalted. Those who convict the innocent will be judged themselves. Their hands will be swapped.

This was good news for the people of Judah back then and it is good news for you today. When you think things are at their worst in our society, know that the kingdom of God is not only coming; it's here. It's not here in all it's fullness but it's here when you work towards justice and alleviating oppression. You bear witness to the truth that the hands have been swapped!

Message Point 3: The shame of God's people will be reversed (vv. 22–24)
Sometimes it's hard to continue to serve God and live a righteous life. It almost seems like those who do the wrong thing are winning. And on top of that many people who claim to serve God do some outlandish things. It can make you ashamed. Here Isaiah says the shame of God's people will be removed. They will no longer have to hold their heads down. God will reverse everything they are feeling now when they see the children of Abraham gathered into His family by faith.

And this same thing is happening today. When you look at what God is doing around the world, you can see how God has swapped the hands of so many who were trapped in bondage and sin. And you know what God has done in your own life. He's reversed your shame and given you joy and acceptance and hope!

THAT'LL PREACH

UNO is such a fast-paced and unpredictable game. Everything can change in an instant. This is the way life is. Sometimes it looks like God is smiling on you and you're happy about the hand you've been dealt. At other times you wish you could swap with someone else. Sometimes it looks like there's good in the world and we are making progress against injustice and oppression, and other times it looks like we've taken two steps forward and five steps back. But in moments your situation and the rest of the world looks bleak, hold on to the truth that the game is rigged. You already know the outcome. Ultimately we win!

CONCLUSION

The kingdom of God is about the reversal of the kingdom of Satan. It is a now and not yet thing but we already see it working, even in the present, and hope to see the full reversal when Jesus returns. When Jesus was on the cross, the enemy thought he was winning at this cosmic game but little did he know that Jesus gave us a swap hands card. He traded places with us so that our positions could be reversed! Not just our position but the position of so many others who are losing in life. We are called to give them a swap hands card so their lives can be changed!

NOTES

_____

_____

_____

_____

_____

_____

_____

You Can't Handle The Truth!

By Allen Reynolds

Lesson Theme	Unit Theme	Scripture
Jeremiah: The Suffering Preacher	Courageous Prophets of Change	Jeremiah 38:14–23

INTRODUCTION

Have you ever seen someone getting ready to make a bad decision? They may have told you about their situation, complained about it, sympathized over it, and then said, "So what do you think I should do?" You know they are getting ready to debate with whatever you have to say. But you know you would feel bad if you didn't at least speak the truth with love. You want to say to your friend, "You say you want the truth, but you can't handle the truth!" That is exactly how Jeremiah felt when Zedekiah the king came to ask for his prophetic wisdom during a critical situation.

MESSAGE POINTS

Message Point 1: Foolish or Faithful? (Jeremiah 38:14–16)
Jeremiah was reasonably cautious. People say, "Fool me once, shame on you; fool me twice, shame on me," and Jeremiah was embodying that skepticism. He had been threatened with death, lied about, and persecuted for speaking the truth of God before. Now King Zedekiah was coming to him again for advice. Jeremiah couldn't help but state the obvious; he had seen this movie before. If Jeremiah told the king the truth, not only would he not listen, but he would also try to have him killed for bringing him more bad news. Zedekiah promised he would react differently this time, that he thought he could handle the truth and obey the word of the Lord through Jeremiah.

Message Point 2: Disgrace or Death? (vv. 17–19)
Jeremiah delivers the harsh truth from the Lord. The Lord is telling Zedekiah to surrender to his Babylonian enemies. If he surrenders, then he and his family will live, but if he doesn't surrender, they will die while the city is destroyed. This is the last advice any king wants. Not only will he lose his power, his throne, and his land. But he must also choose between losing either his dignity or his life. Zedekiah is also afraid that if he surrenders, his foreign enemies will let enemies from his own kingdom kill him anyway. Jeremiah did not want to deliver this bad news. But he was obedient to answer truthfully on behalf of the Lord. Then Zedekiah has to trust the word of God from Jeremiah more than he trusts what he sees as reasonable in his hopeless situation.

Message Point 3: Save Face or Save Family? (vv. 20–23)
Jeremiah clarifies the prophetic scenario. If Zedekiah doesn't surrender and obey the word of the Lord, he will lose his dignity before he loses his life anyway. If he doesn't obey God, then the Babylonians will take all of the women from his house along with his children as slaves and spoil, and his own family will make fun of Zedekiah as he is dragged away and his city burned down. But if he obeys the word of the Lord, then God will preserve him and his family even though he will lose his power. Sometimes we must choose the mercy of survival instead of

the pride that means our death. God can keep us even in the midst of our defeats. It is better to go with God than to try to save ourselves in pride every time.

THAT'LL PREACH

A little boy named Xavier heard that another boy, Marcus, was talking about him behind his back. Marcus was saying that Xavier was dirty and poor because he had been wearing the same shoes all year. The little boy decided he would challenge the other boy to a fight. Rumor spread that Xavier wanted to fight, and Marcus told him to meet at the park after school. Xavier's older sister told him to go straight home, that his mom had a surprise for him. She refused to tell him what the surprise was. The little boy was hesitant. If he didn't show up for the fight with Marcus, people would think he was weak. After some convincing, the boy went straight home with his sister. When he got in the apartment, he saw a brand new pair of shoes. His sister had known all along. Xavier showed up the next day, new shoes shining, having defeated his bully without ever lifting a fist.

CONCLUSION

Jeremiah received a harsh word from the Lord. Zedekiah asked him to tell him the truth, but Jeremiah was afraid that he couldn't handle the truth. Despite the difficulty, both the king and the prophet opened themselves to God's truth more than their fears. As a result, the wisdom of God was made clear: to survive Zedekiah would have to sacrifice his pride to save his life and his family. Jeremiah would have to choose once again to fear God more than man. We too are called to obey God, to tell hard truths, and to receive hard truths, because in the end, the truth will always prevail even when it's uncomfortable. So can you handle the truth?

NOTES

_____

_____

_____

_____

_____

_____

_____

_____

_____

_____

_____

_____

U-Turn!

By Penelope White, MCEd.

Lesson Theme	Unit Theme	Scripture
Ezekiel: Street Preacher to the Exiles	Courageous Prophets of Change	Ezekiel 18:1–9, 30–32

INTRODUCTION

Debating, rationalization, plausible explanations, intellectualizing, justifying, vindication—these are as old as the first humans created by God in the Garden of Eden. Fallen humanity looks outward for an excuse, refusing to humbly take inner inventory too many times. Such was the case in our Scripture reading today. The prophet makes the clarion call to God's people that each individual person is responsible for and rewarded by God for their own doings. We know from the study of God's Word and our life experience that God desires His highest creation to be reconciled unto Himself. He went the distance to provide and secure this. It is His heart's cry that none should perish!

MESSAGE POINTS

Message Point 1: Nothing is new under the sun (Ezekiel 18:1–2)

The rebellious nation ancient Israel (and ours) chooses to blame previous generations for their predicament. In our reading today, God's people are suffering the dire consequences of their own misdoings. Yet, there is this murmuring, finger-pointing, fault-finding against the ancestors. They raise the argument citing a portion of Scripture written before: "The fathers have eaten a sour grape, and the children's teeth are set on edge" (Jeremiah 31:28–30). The people lean to their own understanding and claim that they are being punished for past sins of their fathers. Used out of context, the Bible has been twisted and mishandled attempting to justify many evils throughout the ages.

Message Point 2: Not my mother, not my father... (vv. 3–4)

At this time, God makes a clear declaration saying Israel will no longer be able to use this saying, for everyone is personally responsible and accountable for their individual actions. God meets the people's complaint of bearing generational burdens and hardships with His response: They shall no more say (that is, they shall have no more occasion to say) that God visits the iniquity of the parents upon the children. Gone are the days of pointing to others as the cause of our dilemma, crisis, or consequence.

Message Point 3: But it's me, O Lord (vv. 30–32)

God will individually judge each Israelite. Their sin and disgusting deeds will not live! No, they will not. All their good deeds will be forgotten, and they will be put to death because of their individual sins. God poses a thought-provoking question again, "Have I any pleasure at all that the wicked should die? saith the Lord GOD: and not that he should return from his ways, and live?" (v. 23). Although God is perfectly just when He chooses to impose judgment, He would always prefer His children to repent and return to a relationship with Him.

When you travel on an unfamiliar route, what do you do? Yes, you have GPS, Waze, Bluetooth, turn-by-turn instructions. Every app is in place. You're tech-savvy, trip savvy. I want to know if we ever get distracted, of course, detoured, in a word: lost! We started just fine, ears tuned, eyes and mind focused, gas tank full, but now that needle is hugging E, confusion has set in, and our ears hear mixed messages asking who is to blame! Really? Christian living is a journey—some may even say a trip. So stop tripping and know that we—all of us—must R.E.P.E.N.T.:

Return to our starting point (Jesus) and the cross, **E**very day, to **P**ray **E**arly in the morning (Psalms 5:3), and make the **N**ecessary **T**urns (even if it's a U-turn).

CONCLUSION

Yahweh remains a holy God and must deal with those who are hardened by their sins. Is there any hope? Any good news? Yes! There is the best news ever—God is always ready to receive, embrace, welcome those who are humbled by their sins and then take the crucial steps to turn away from them.

Who among us does not need refreshing, refueling, regrouping, reconciliation, restoration, rejuvenation, replenishing, refocusing with the true GPS: God's Positioning System? Each one of us stands in desperate need! Let us repent, let's turn, let's u-turn to our faithful and forgiving Father who longs to have us connected, close, comforted, guided safely by Him! For He has said, "I am the Way" (from John 14:6).

What amazing love! The Master of the universe paid the ultimate price so we could be called His own and guided to our destination: Jesus, the Anointed One!

NOTES

_____

_____

_____

_____

_____

_____

_____

_____

_____

_____

_____

The Persistence of Grace

By Rev. Larry Kirk

Lesson Theme	Unit Theme	Scripture
Jonah: Do the Right Thing	Courageous Prophets of Change	Jonah 3

INTRODUCTION

In the closing minutes of class at seminary, we discussed whether one could ever say that God was judging a nation or a city when catastrophe strikes. The previous Sunday, Hurricane Katrina had hit New Orleans; the following Sunday was the anniversary of September 11. Some students seemed confident these things are God's judgments; others were just as convinced that we cannot know that. We ran out of time before we ended the discussion. Well, anyone can indulge in speculation. For Christians, the only trustworthy foundation for our faith is revelation. What Jonah learned about judgment and grace is useful for us in all of life.

MESSAGE POINTS

Message Point 1: God's Grace is Persistent (Jonah 3:1–2)

Notice how Jonah 3 begins: "And the word of the LORD came unto Jonah the second time" (v. 1). Why did God send Jonah to Nineveh? The answer is because of His grace and compassion. Part of the message of Jonah is how out of touch we can be with the heart of God. Jonah wanted to wipe Nineveh off the map, but God wanted Nineveh to experience His grace. The last words in the book are a question from God: "Should not I spare Nineveh, that great city?" (4:11).

The prophet Nahum describes the sins of Nineveh. "Woe to the bloody city! it is all full of lies and robbery; the prey departeth not" (Nahum 3:1). Nahum 3:4 indicts the people of Nineveh for violence, lust, prostitution, and witchcraft. The book of Jonah tells us that He had concern, compassion, grace, and abounding love for Nineveh. God does judge sin, but not all suffering is judgment. God's people are not exempt from the natural calamities that affect all people in a fallen world (cf. Romans 8). God's people are called to show kindness to those who suffer, without regard to what they deserve.

Not just one or two cities deserve judgment but the whole world, the city of mankind, and everyone in it (Romans 3:1–20). What is God's response? Ultimately what He does is send not just a reluctant prophet but His own Son. The Scripture says, "For God sent not his Son into the world to condemn the world; but that the world through him might be saved" (John 3:17). Christ came not just with a call to repentance but with an act of redemption. In our place on the cross, Christ actually suffered the judgment we deserve. The same grace and abounding love that sent Jonah to Nineveh sent Jesus to die and rise again for you and me.

Message Point 2: God's Grace Calls Us to Repentance (vv. 4–5)

Repentance involves both faith and humility toward God (v. 5). Notice verse 5 says, "So the people of Nineveh believed God." They declared a fast, an act of humility, and they put on sackcloth. Inputting on sackcloth, you were humbling yourself before God and submitting yourself to Him. That's the response we all need to bring to God. It doesn't matter what you have suffered, or lost, or done, or failed to do. Repentance is not just for sinful unbelievers but for self-righteous saints. That's part of the story. Against the backdrop of the sinful city stands the self-righteous prophet. He also needs repentance. Jonah 3 begins: "And the word of the LORD came unto Jonah the second time" (v. 1). These almost exactly parallel the opening words of the book. God is telling Jonah he needs to start over again. He was self-righteous and self-centered. There is persistent grace for Jonah.

Message Point 3: God Is Always Ready to Save (v. 6–10)
After Jonah preached to the people of Nineveh (3:1–4), they turned away from their wickedness. Verse 10 says, "God saw their works, that they turned from their evil way" and spared them from the judgment that had awaited them. God is always ready to save us. His mercy far exceeds any sin that we can imagine. Isaiah says, "Let the wicked forsake his way, and the unrighteous man his thoughts; let him return to the LORD, and He will have mercy on him; and to our God, for He will abundantly pardon" (Isaiah 55:7). And Peter would later add that God is longsuffering toward us and "not willing that any should perish, but that all should come to repentance" (2 Peters 3:9). The people of Nineveh experienced God's mercy firsthand, and we can as well. All we need to do is turn away from those things that masquerade as true life and fulfillment and blind us from seeing God's love for us.

THAT'LL PREACH

It seems the hardest phrase to say is "I'm sorry." We never like to own up to our mistakes. We want to explain why we did what we did. We want to hear the other person say sorry first. We want everyone to just move on and forget it. But every so often a message comes along that encourages us that this is the time to apologize. The message reminds us how important personal relationships are. It reminds us that we're better than this petty disagreement. It asks for confession and holds out for the promise of forgiveness. Let this message be that message right now in your life.

CONCLUSION

Maybe you've got 40 days, 40 weeks, months, years? I don't know. But there comes a time when your heart is hardened or the season of grace is gone or the kids are grown up or the marriage is over. Or you've died. It is too late one way or another. Maybe these were your 40 minutes. I don't know. We all need to pray, "Lord, search me and know me and show me anywhere and everywhere I need to repent. Give me the grace to respond in glad obedience to Your Word to me today."

NOTES

_____

_____

_____

_____

_____

_____

_____

Unbothered Faith

By Dwight Radcliff

Lesson Theme	Unit Theme	Scripture
Why Do you Worry?	Jesus Teaches about Faith	Matthew 6:25–34

INTRODUCTION

It's easy to be distracted by the term "worry" when reading this passage of Scripture. These ten verses mention worry six times so, of course, we would naturally focus on worry. But I think that's part of the trap! It seems as though Matthew's point is that worry robs—or at least distracts—the believer from having faith in God. When we make "worry" the key idea of this passage, we miss one of the major points that Matthew makes about the teaching of Jesus throughout his entire Gospel. What if the key to understanding this passage is not about focusing on worry itself? What if the key is that this particular type of anxiety robs the believer from the ability to believe—to have faith? Ultimately, we can't allow worry to distract us from what's most important. This passage is about walking in faith, unbothered by worry, passionately seeking the Kingdom of God.

MESSAGE POINTS

Message Point 1: What Worry Won't Do (Matthew 6:25–30)

During His famous Sermon on the Mount, Jesus engages in teaching on faith, disguised in a conversation about worry. Jesus, the Master Teacher, knew that the role that worry, anxiety, and concern played in the people of that day's lives. We could—and should—say much today about the devastating effects of stress and anxiety in our time. Jesus begins by deconstructing the concept of worry. He engages His audience by highlighting that worry, in and of itself, can't actually increase or add anything to a person's life (v. 27).

Worry doesn't clothe or feed anyone. The very things that we need (food and shelter) are not provided by our habits of worry. What we need, worry won't provide! The proof is in the fact that the birds of the air (v. 26) and the lilies of the field (v. 28). Not even the glorious wealth of Solomon can compare to the beautiful splendor of God's provision.

Message Point 2: What Worry Will Do (vv. 31-32)

In fact, it isn't the negative aspects of worry that are the most dangerous. Rather, it is what worry does. Worry produces a belief system that runs contrary to what Jesus is preaching and teaching. The entire Sermon on the Mount can be seen as a counter-cultural shift in the way we understand God and pursue community with people. In this sense, Jesus is telling followers that worrying and obsessing over things (that God already knows they need) will have them end up like Gentiles.

This behavior of obsessing and worrying goes directly against a life that is rooted in faith in God. The believer cannot live like non-believers who do not trust God. The believer must have confidence that God knows what they need. The believer must have the confidence that God will supply that need. Worry is a viral infection in the life of faith. It distracts and bothers the believer's trust in God.

Message Point 3: Why Faith is the Focus (v. 30)
Faith is a big deal in Matthew's Gospel, a big deal! So much so, that on at least four different occasions he shows Jesus proclaiming that the disciples had "little faith" (8:26, 14:31, 16:8, 17:20). Matthew goes even further and proclaims that the greatest faith Jesus saw was in a centurion (chapter 8) and a Syro-Phoenician woman (whom Matthew called a Canaanite, chapter 15). For Matthew, it is often those outsiders that have demonstrated the greatest confidence and trust in God. Both of these incidents happen after Jesus's sermon here.

I would argue that the focus of this passage is not in the repetitive use of worry within this passage, but the bold assertion of faith in verse 30. If you can see and consider how God clothes and feeds those animals who are not distracted by our cares and concerns, then why can't you see and consider that God will take care of the one who trusts in Him? To lack confidence in God's provision is to have little faith. To lack trust in God's care is to have little faith. And Matthew will show us repeatedly that we must trust God.

THAT'LL PREACH

Horses have pretty good peripheral vision. They can also be spooked or can veer off track. Before a horse runs in a race, its trainer puts blinders around its eyes to divert its attention to the race and the finish line. With the blinders on the hourse is less distracted and unbothered by the other things happening around them.

Sometimes this Christian race requires us to wear blinders. Just because you have blinders on doesn't mean that you're not in the race. It doesn't mean that the competition is not fierce. It doesn't mean that the dangers are not real. It simply means that in order for me to run this race I've been given to the best of my ability, I will have to deny some of my sensory perceptions so that I can seek the Kingdom of God! Yes, there are real worries and concerns about the world we live in. But I cannot let my faith be bothered to the point where I forget to trust God.

CONCLUSION

A faith that is bothered is little faith. It is the faith that forced the disciples to ask seemingly silly questions of Jesus, distracting them from the big ideas and the main objectives. Is your faith so bothered by fear and worry that you've forgotten to trust God? I invite you to go outside. I invite you to look at the birds and the flowers. They should remind your faith that God still cares.

NOTES

_____

_____

_____

_____

_____

_____

Are You In or Out?

By Dr. Cheryl Price

Lesson Theme	Unit Theme	Scripture
Why Are You Afraid?	Jesus Teaches about Faith	Matthew 8:23–27

INTRODUCTION

In our Scripture text for today, we find the disciples, many of them experienced fisherman and expert sailboat navigators, leaving Capernaum with Jesus, and sailing across the Sea of Galilee to the Gentile Gadarene area. Jesus had healed many people before they boarded the boat, including Peter's sick mother-in-law. The disciples had witnessed Jesus' many miracles and even the faith of a non-believer, a Roman officer, who believed Jesus could heal his very sick servant. Yet, they doubted Jesus.

MESSAGE POINTS

Message Point 1: Following Jesus is Costly (Matthew 8:22)

We are introduced to two disciples who want to follow Jesus. The first one we meet in verse 21. Disciple number one declares that he will follow Jesus whereever He goes. Jesus tells him that if he wants to follow, the cost is greater than he knows. He tells this disciple that the cost is so great, He does not have a home or a place to sleep, even though foxes and birds do. "You can follow Me," He seems to say, "but the cost to live and do as I do makes for a hard life." In verse 22, we meet the second disciple who wants to follow Jesus. Jesus basically tells this disciple, "You too can follow Me, but you have to go now." The second disciple is surprised by Jesus' quick response. He wants to follow Jesus but says he needs to bury his father. Jesus tells him, "Follow me; and let the dead bury their dead" (v. 22). Jesus accepts no excuses from the disciples or us to not follow Him. This may make us feel uncomfortable, but Jesus gives us His all. We should give Jesus our all.

Message Point 2: Following Jesus is Frightening (vv. 23–25)

We do not know the disciples that we encountered in Matthew 8:21–22, but we are very familiar with Jesus' twelve disciples in verses 23–25. These disciples are the same ones who Jesus has been training in divine discipleship. Jesus has shown them who He is in multiple ways. They walked, talked, ate, and dealt with difficult situations together. A strong brotherhood had been formed until it was broken by fear and faithlessness. The disciples no longer believed or trusted Jesus to care for them when they found themselves with Jesus in a boat and a horrendous storm had overtaken them. They did what any other God-fearing believer would do, they woke Jesus up. Shaking with fear and asking Jesus to save them from drowning. Why would Jesus let them drown and He is in the boat with them? They forgot who Jesus is. When we are afraid, we too want Jesus to deliver us from the storms in our lives.

Message Point 3: Following Jesus is Calming (v. 27)

Remember, the storm is ferocious, and Jesus is asleep. The disciples were unable to battle the storm and take command of the ship. The storm had violently overtaken them. They wanted and needed Jesus. After the disciples awaken Jesus, He responds to their fears by questioning their fears. Jesus tells the winds and the waves to stop terrible behavior, and immediately they become calm. The disciples were shocked and wondered who Jesus really is. Jesus knows that we are afraid but wants us to follow and trust Him. Trust Jesus and talk to Him like you would to a friend. Remember in challenging times, hold on because there is someone or something God will send or has sent to help you. It is hard at times, but you can do it.

THAT'LL PREACH

There was a picture I saw going around on social media. It was joking about how dogs can have selective hearing. A burglar breaks into the house, and the dog's asleep. A fire engine goes wailing by, and the dog's asleep. Doorbell rings, and the dog's still asleep. But if they hear a cheese wrapper? Well then, they're up and in your face in a second! The dog knows what's important. I find just as much humor in the disciples' situation here too. Rain starts pouring down, Jesus is asleep. Winds pick up, Jesus is still asleep. Waves crash over the boat, Jesus is still asleep. But when His disciples call and truly start having a crisis of faith, Jesus is up right away, and instantly solves the problem. He knows what's important. Jesus had no worries about His personal safety. But whenever we ask Him for help, He is always ready to help us in our times of crisis.

CONCLUSION

We have read the stories in the Bible: all of Jesus' miracles of healing, all His wise and authoritative teaching. We have seen Him work in our friends' lives and even our own. Not one of us here today has gotten this far in life without knowing they have experienced a "God moment." The question is when life gets hard, will we still believe? When the storms of life rage, will we fear we are going to drown? Or will we pray to our God to help us, who can solve any problem with a simple command?

NOTES

_____

_____

_____

_____

_____

_____

_____

_____

_____

_____

_____

Help From the Healer

By Pastor Rosalyn Bates

Lesson Theme	**Unit Theme**	**Scripture**
Healed by Faith	Jesus Teaches About Faith	Matthew 9:18–26

INTRODUCTION

People who have had a chronic illness or cared about someone who has one are aware that severe ailments are life-altering. Most, if not, all of the activities of daily living become more challenging and often demand more time than anticipated. Completing basic, everyday tasks also can require strategies and detailed planning. Having a disease impacts the ailing person and those who love and care for them. The Gospel of Matthew, where our text is found, aims to persuade its audience that Jesus Christ is indeed the long-awaited Messiah. Jesus Christ is the Anointed One who is sent to restore what is in disrepair and the One who has authority over the oppression of sickness and disease. Matthew's Gospel presents Jesus to a largely Jewish audience and depicts Jesus as the fulfillment of Jewish law and the prophets. In this particular passage, Jesus returns to His own city by boat, having just honored the faith of four friends by healing their paralyzed loved one. He addresses the ailments of two females, one older and one younger.

MESSAGE POINTS

Message Point 1: Faith Against the Odds (Matthew 9:18–19)
Jesus responds to the synagogue ruler's faith on behalf of his daughter when the odds are against him. This ruler in the synagogue, Jairus, stands out among many who approach Jesus with a request for a miracle. This ruler is one of few people in the Scriptures who directly states to Jesus that he believes Jesus could raise someone from the dead. Despite the death of his only daughter, his faith prompts him to come to Jesus and worship Him. Even though his situation is what many would perhaps describe as a done deal, a wrap, a lost cause, too late, or beyond repair, Jairus's faith is strong enough to compel him to seek out Jesus, worship Him, and make his request known. By faith, Jairus understands that Jesus' power truly rules and overrides natural occurrences. Jairus courageously invites Jesus to his home and consequently into his desperate situation. How often do we boldly face the odds with our faith, worship Jesus, and invite Him into our most dire circumstance?

Message Point 2: Faith to Risk Exposure (vv. 20–22)
Jesus recognizes the woman's faith as she risks being seen in her pursuit of healing. The unnamed woman in this text has suffered from horrible hemorrhages for 12 long years. She has been responsible to keep her multiple appointments for treatment to address this health issue. This woman invested in her health such that her funds were depleted by medical bills. Yet instead of her condition improving with time and specialized care, her condition worsened. She believes that being exposed if only to Jesus and his healing power, is worth the risk. No one knows she is in the crowd until she approaches Jesus from behind and touches the fringe of His clothes. This minimal contact has maximum results. As she believed, her hemorrhage stops with one quick, but a life-saving encounter. She would have preferred to keep a low profile and avoid public exposure so that no one, including Je-

83

sus, would see her at her absolute worst in the progression of the disease. Yet Jesus feels her touch Him among the pressing crowds. Her faith caused her to risk being seen by Jesus and others, this time, to the glory of God.

Message Point 3: Faith That Displaces Unbelievers (vv. 23–26)
Jesus displaces the people around Jairus who are doubtful. Once Jesus arrives at Jairus's home, He finds people in a state of mourning. He encourages Jairus to not be afraid, and Jesus is the first person to stand in solidarity with the faith of Jairus. He tells him to only believe, to have faith only. Then Jesus instructs the doubters, the sneering, the harassing and the mocking crowd of people to leave, go outside and away from Jairus's daughter. This daughter was close to going down in history as another statistic of the times by dying at a young age. However, her father's faith compels him to ask Jesus for divine intervention. Jesus literally put the unbelievers out of the space where the daughter was before He entered it. Then Jesus took Jairus' daughter's hand and told her to get up. Sometimes protecting the strength of our faith means ensuring that our environment is occupied by people who will similarly trust and believe God with us.

THAT'LL PREACH

Both modern and ancient health practices recognize the medicinal value of balms. A balm by definition is a sweet-smelling oil that comes from tropical trees, used to make creams that heal wounds and reduce pain. It is a restorative agent, ointment, or preparation that heals and soothes the skin. A balm often has a fragrance, and the fragrance of the balm eliminates the odor that some wounds release. In Jeremiah 8:21–22, the prophet Jeremiah, seeing the wounded condition of people toward God, asks the questions, "Is there no balm in Gilead; is there no physician there?" Gilead was a place that was known for its healing medicine. The people's spiritual sickness was deep, but God, the Physician, could heal their spiritual sickness and restore them if only they would apply the balm through their obedience.

CONCLUSION

When our faith looks up to the Lord Jesus Christ for healing, we summon His mighty power to defeat the odds that are against us. He sees us at our weakest and worst moments, and He will love us from there into a state of strength and wholeness. Although our faith in Jesus may initially cause others to mock us, our trust in Him makes room for the miraculous.

NOTES

_____

_____

_____

_____

_____

_____

_____

Jesus Will Meet You in the Storm

By Rev. Jaimie Crumley

Lesson Theme	Unit Theme	Scripture
Why Do You Doubt?	Jesus Teaches about Faith	Matthew 14:22–33

INTRODUCTION

Have you ever been battered by the storms of life? Maybe you received a diagnosis that left you reeling. Or, perhaps you survived a natural disaster but lost many of the things you hold dear. Maybe you are grappling with the death of a friend or family member. Maybe you suffered through a season of financial instability. In the trying seasons of our lives, we can become seized by fear because we do not know how we are going to survive. We often feel hopeless until we look up and see that Jesus is reaching out His hands to us. Jesus will guide us through our storms.

MESSAGE POINTS

Message Point 1: Far from the Peaceful Shore (Matthew 14:22–24)

Jesus will go to great lengths to teach us about faith. In Matthew 14, Jesus sent the disciples to their boat while He went to a mountain by Himself to pray. The mountain appears consistently throughout the Gospel of Matthew to connect Jesus' ministry to that of Moses in the Torah. While the disciples sat and waited for Jesus, a storm came, and their boat drifted further from the shore. Like a good pastor, teacher, leader, parent, or grandparent who is trying to help us grow, Jesus knows that sometimes we only learn to thrive when we think we are all alone and must survive on our own. When you are going through trials, consider how you can learn, grow, and be changed even by the circumstances that feel unbearable. Through it all, know that Jesus is right there, guiding, supporting, and loving you.

Message Point 2: "Do Not Be Afraid" (vv. 25–27)

"Do not be afraid." It is a phrase that recurs throughout Scripture as early as humanity's first encounters with the presence of God. We often fear the presence of God for two reasons. First, we fear God's presence because we are ashamed. After eating from the Tree of the Knowledge of Good and Evil, Adam and Eve hid from God because they realized they were naked, and they were ashamed. Second, we fear the presence of God because we do not know what life-shifting demands God might make of us. As early as Genesis, God commanded humans to uproot their lives in service to the will of God. Throughout human history, God has reassured us that there is no need to fear because we are loved by an Almighty Savior. The next time you feel afraid, take heart and call on the One who will not leave you.

Message Point 3: Withstanding Life's Strong Winds (vv. 28–33)

Jesus calls us to come out and meet Him on the water even as the storms of life rage. As believers, we often rest in the assurance that Jesus will protect us no matter what. We believe that when we walk toward Jesus, we will not falter. This passage reminds us that as we grow in our faith, Jesus entrusts us with greater responsibility.

Trusting Jesus does not mean that we will no longer encounter storms in our lives. But, as Christ-followers, we are called to collaborate with Him in the building of a godly Kingdom here on earth. Even when life's storms and heavy winds assail us, we can keep our feet planted on the promise that God is still with us. God will never fail us.

THAT'LL PREACH

We live in a world plagued by cataclysmic natural disasters, mass murders, war, and genocide. Not to mention the challenges we face every day in our neighborhoods, workplaces, schools, churches, and families! Feeling afraid is a natural reaction to the storms that seem to assail us daily. Yet, we also encounter so many reasons to have hope. Our children grow in faith and create rich lives for themselves. Our churches thrive and help support our communities. We build lasting relationships with our family members, friends, and neighbors. God keeps pouring out blessings on us. As Alice Walker's protagonist Celie proclaims in response to those who belittle her in *The Color Purple*, "But, I'm here." Tell the storms in your life that no matter how they rage, you are still here by the grace of God. Have faith; Jesus will meet you in the middle of your storm to guide you safely to the shore.

CONCLUSION

Jesus allows us to learn and grow in our faith. Although the world around us can sometimes seem like a frightening place, as Christ-followers we can take heart because Jesus is with us. Even when we feel distant from His presence, Jesus is always right there, just waiting for us to call His name. So, deal with life's challenges head-on. Jesus will meet you in the middle of your storm.

NOTES

_____

_____

_____

_____

_____

_____

_____

_____

_____

_____

_____

_____

_____

_____

Lessons From The Lepers

By Joshua Edmon

Lesson Theme	Unit Theme	Scripture
An Attitude of Gratitude	Jesus Teaches About Faith	Leviticus 13:45–46; Luke 17:11–19

INTRODUCTION

Have you ever learned lessons from people you never thought you would learn from? Maybe it was someone you didn't know who taught you something you hold on to today. Or maybe a person who was considered an outcast gave you a nugget of wisdom that radically changed your life. When I was growing up, we had a man who lived in our neighborhood who impacted our community. His name was Mr. McFarland. "Mr. Mac," as we affectionately called him, wasn't the best-dressed man, nor was he the most articulate, but he was a servant. Mr. McFarland taught people how to garden, how to fix cars, and how to repair homes. Mr. Mac did not have a college degree, yet he taught many people. One lesson Mr. McFarland's life taught me was you don't have to be the most educated person to teach and impact people. The reality is lessons come from the most peculiar people. In this message, we learn from a very interesting group of people, the lepers.

MESSAGE POINTS

Message Point 1: A Passionate Plea (Luke 17:11–14)

Jesus is traveling through Samaria and Galilee. Now, when He comes into this village, ten men with leprosy meet Him. These men with leprosy didn't come close to Jesus because according to Leviticus 13:45-46 they had to wear clothes that were torn, not take care of their hair, and wherever they went they had to cry out, "Unclean! Unclean!" They also had to live alone. They were the outcasts of society. Yet, the lepers encountered a merciful master and their plea was, "Have mercy on us." Jesus responds. The text tells us that Jesus told them to, "Go shew yourselves unto the priests" (v. 14). Responding to Jesus' command, they were cleansed! Sometimes you have to have just enough courage and forget about the cultural norms and make your plea before God to receive from Him. Here's the deal, Jesus is not bound to cultural norms. Jesus' power reaches beyond all of our broken-ness, pain, and hurt. Jesus doesn't reject our request but responds to our needs! All we have to do is make a passionate plea and move when He tells us to move.

Message Point 2: A Powerful Praise (vv. 15–16)

Let me pause right here to ask you a question: How would you respond if you were healed?

Well, as we pick up in this story, we see only one man, a Samaritan, returned to Jesus with powerful praise! The leper gave Jesus thanks and praise for the healing He had performed in his life. The praise this man gave was loud, he did not hold back, he raised his voice in praise. He even fell at Jesus' feet and thanked Him. The praise he gave God through Jesus was no ordinary praise, it wasn't cute or sophisticated. The praise he lifted up came from a heart of gratitude for what Jesus had done for him. This man, a Samaritan, who was considered in those times as one who lacked faith in God, had enough sense to praise God for what He had done. Let's be like this

Samaritan and praise God for who He is and for what He has done. Has He saved you? You should be giving Him powerful praise! Has God delivered you? Then, you should be giving Him powerful praise!

Message Point 3: A Problem & Pronouncement (vv. 17–19)
Nine other men had received the same healing, but they did not come back to give God thanks! Perhaps, they just went on with life forgetting that just a few moments before this encounter with Jesus, they were considered the filth of society. Maybe the other nine wanted to show family members and friends who had abandoned them that they were well now. Whatever the case was, they failed to give God praise for what He had done, and Jesus had a problem with that. Because he came back, the foreigner (this word often meant "pagan" or "heathen") is praised and is given a pronouncement. Jesus says to this Samaritan, "Thy faith hath made thee whole" (v. 19). Jesus wants to heal us, and He wants to set us free. But when Jesus does amazing work in our lives, let's not be the kind of people Jesus has a problem with, because we forget to praise Him. Let's learn from the one leper who came back to God and praised Him. When we do this, we will hear God pronounce over us, "Our faith has made us well!"

THAT'LL PREACH

My wife is amazing! She loves me and my family with a fierce love, and I am so grateful for how she both leads and serves. I've noticed something over the past few months that has bothered me a bit though. Let me explain what I mean, my children say things like, "Mom, can you make me a peanut butter and jelly sandwich." And, my wife being the person she is, does exactly what they ask for. The one thing that bothers me, though, is the fact that my children never or rarely say thank you for making the sandwich. It's almost as if they think that's just what Mom is supposed to do. Let's not be like that with God. When God does something for us, let's not forget to express thanks and praise for the things He has done for us! Let's be like the one leper who came back to tell God thank you. Our God is generous, and we should be generous with our praise!

CONCLUSION

What we learn from the lepers is that we can call out to God with a passionate plea! When we call out to God and He answers us, we should give Him powerful praise. Now when we fail to give God praise for what He has done, God takes issue; He has a problem with that. But, when we do give God praise, we receive a positive pronouncement from God. Therefore, let's remember to continue to call out to God. Now, when God answers, let's always remember to give Him praise and thanksgiving!

NOTES

_____

_____

_____

_____

_____

_____

_____

Power to Live

By Joshua Edmon

Lesson Theme	Unit Theme	Scripture
The Power of the Gospel	Faith and Salvation	Romans 1:8–17

INTRODUCTION

Paul's letter to the Romans is probably the most well-reasoned treatise on the Gospel in Scripture. In it, he discusses the Gospel concerning the law, to prophecy, and the universal needs of mankind. The great question Paul seems to be on a quest to answer in Romans is this, "What is the meaning and purpose of the Gospel?" This question is one of supreme importance to the Christian. We often focus attention on sharing the Gospel message and maintaining the behaviors we should demonstrate in light of the Gospel we have believed. But, before we can effectively preach the "what" of the Gospel or live out the "how," we must be fully convinced of the "why" of the Gospel. Before we share it and to live it, we have to experience the blessing of the Gospel. In these early verses of Paul's great letter, the apostle lays out the compelling purpose and transcendent blessing of the Gospel and it is this: the Gospel is the power to live.

MESSAGE POINTS

Message Point 1: Faith Builds Reputation (Romans 1:8–9)
The first area of life that we see addressed in the text is the external life. If we're not careful, this external impact of the Gospel could easily be missed. Paul mentions to the Roman Christians how their faith is being, "spoken of throughout the whole world" (v. 8). At this point in history, Rome was the center of the Western world. Art, philosophy, and politics were regularly outsourced. But with so much to talk about from Rome, people had taken notice and shared the story of the profound impact that the Gospel had on these Romans. We all want to build a strong reputation. The power of the Gospel to transform a life is always a compelling narrative. Christian, if you want to be known for something, be known for the transformative impact Jesus has had on your life.

Message Point 2: Faith Breeds Relationships (vv. 10–15)
One of the impacts of the Gospel is that it brings us into a relationship with all believers; past, present, and future. In fact, the Scripture tells us that we are grafted into Abraham's line (Romans 11:17), we are made "joint-heirs with Christ" (Romans 8:17), members of the body of Christ (1 Corinthians 12:27). Paul writes with affection and deep concern for these Roman Christians even though he has never met them. The apostle talks about the sense of obligation he feels to preach the Gospel to the "Greeks" (the sophisticated, wealthier Hellenists) and the "Barbarians" (poor, ethnically diverse, and less metropolitan). Paul desires as the apostle to the Gentiles to encourage the faith of these Roman believers, but at the same time, he understands that the faith of these lay people will also encourage his own faith. If we will allow it, faith in Jesus will take us everywhere and bring us into relationships with all kinds of people. Never forget that you have brothers and sisters on the other side of the world that you've never met. Be ever conscious of the fact that the person sitting next to you at a concert or in a movie theater could be family if you share Jesus with them. Nobody is too high up the social ladder and indeed

no one is too far down to bless your own life. The first thing God ever said about man is that "It is not good that the man should be alone" (Genesis 2:18). We all need a relationship, and faith can help us find them.

Message Point 3: Faith Brings Revelation (vv. 16–17)
Praise God for the impact the Gospel has on the external life and interpersonal life! But it would all be for naught were it not for the impact that the Gospel has on the internal and eternal life. The most blessed thing for humanity is to see God more clearly. That is why Moses—when he could have asked God for anything—made this request, "Show me your face!" It is why Solomon asked God, "Teach me your ways." And in the Gospel, the righteousness of God is revealed by faith which produces more faith. How appropriate then that Paul reaches for the prophet Habakkuk standing in the midst of his own adversity crying out to God, "O LORD, how long" (Habakkuk 1:2), and receiving this blessed exhortation, "The just shall live by faith" (Habakkuk 2:4). In all our trials of our soul in life and even life's final trial, faith will be our sustaining principle.

THAT'LL PREACH

Everybody is trying to figure out life. People everywhere are working through the tough questions of life: How do I build a legacy? How do I have good relationships? How do I find inner peace? You may be wrestling with these same questions. Maybe like so many people, you are turning to every self-help expert, university study, and socially conscious entertainer. Allow me to commend to you the Gospel of Jesus Christ. To believe this Gospel is to experience the kind of transformation that makes your life a story worth telling. To believe this Gospel is to be drawn into a divinely orchestrated network of eternal relationships that span every area of society and every corner of the globe. To believe this Gospel is to receive life-sustaining access to the personality of the Godhead. These other sources may seem more contemporary, more relevant, even more sophisticated. But I join with the Apostle Paul in boldly proclaiming that I am not ashamed of this Gospel. It is the power of God.

CONCLUSION

Why the Gospel? The Gospel is not first a message to preach. It certainly is not a set of rules to govern behavior. Above all else, the Gospel is the immeasurable power of Almighty God. And when we connect by faith to that power, it has immense implications for our lives.

NOTES

_____

_____

_____

_____

_____

_____

_____

A God-kind-of Faith... WALK IT!

By Penelope White, MCEd

Lesson Theme	Unit Theme	Scripture
The Faith of Abraham	Faith and Salvation	Romans 4:1–12

INTRODUCTION

Faith is foundational, first, and final in our Christian walk with God. Every single step is taken by faith; not by sight, understanding, or even desire. Without this essential component, it is impossible to please the Lord (Hebrews 11:6). It is given to the believer by God Himself. So, what is this backbone of our relationship with our God? How exactly and when is it acquired? Are there any flesh and bone examples we can consult?

MESSAGE POINTS

Message Point 1: God describes Abraham (Romans 4:1–3)

Abraham, known as the Father of the Faith, serves as our illustration cited in Romans 4:1. He is highly regarded among those Paul is addressing (Jewish believers in Rome). Paul maps out Abraham's situation along with God's reckoning and calling Abraham righteous. He masterfully points out that Abraham, Father of the Faith, has been credited as such not based on some grand work nor any specified ritual; yet God confirms Abraham as being in right standing with Him. Paul asks, "For what saith the scripture? Abraham believed God, and it was counted unto him for righteousness" (Romans 4:3). This must always be the litmus test for all discussion, controversy, and debate. What does the Word of God, the Holy Scriptures, say?

Message Point 2: How is Abraham considered righteous? (vv. 4–8)

This righteousness Paul refers to was—and still is—given by God, through faith, to all who believe. According to Genesis 15, Abraham's belief in God and in what God said supports his righteousness. When God gave His promise and stamped Abraham righteous, Abraham had not yet seen any part of his covenant blessing, yet He believed God. His belief had already led him to pack up and journey far from all that he knew. Abraham had no son and certainly no descendants more numerous than the stars. He believed God. Although he had no land claim in the Promised Land and no promised son, he believed God. Unwavering, unwaning faith is credited as righteousness. It beckoned Abraham to move to begin walking according to all GOD has spoken.

Message Point 3: Not works, but a walk (vv. 9–12)

Paul now approaches the subject of circumcision and non-Jewish believers. Was it this act that made Abraham right with God? God gives Abraham the righteous ID before any outward act on the patriarch's own initiative. The circumcision took place after Abraham was declared righteous, as a sign of his belief in God's commands accompanied by His promises. God has graciously, freely, readily identified Abraham based solely on his belief—no human effort, no godly works, or anything else. This is to emphasize that anyone—circumcised, uncircumcised, Jew, Gentile, moral, immoral, destined to become a heroic figure in the Christian faith or not—can be justified and considered righteous by faith or belief in God. So, Abraham is indeed the father of all who follow in his steps of believing God. He walked trusting that what God said would come to pass. Abraham's fixed focus was on all that God had spoken to him, that it would indeed manifest. Though it seemed impossible based on circumstances, human reasoning, and natural outcomes, Abraham walked, continued, pressed, and moved toward the fulfillment of every promise.

THAT'LL PREACH

Those among us who are frequently immobilized, bound, stuck in a place of calculating all of the how, when, where, why of God's instructive voice are to be encouraged with this: Believe God. Let's keep the main thing, the first thing. No need to wait for thunderbolts or great exploits. God's talk says you are right with Him because you believe Him. When the tailor-made Word of our Lord comes to us, the only response that brings honor and satisfaction to Him is our walking in that command. Faith says, God's talk is my walk...now walk it!

We may not always be required to pack up all our belongings and leave for a physical place we know not of like Abraham, but God's talk may speak to us about praying for those who are in leadership with whom we have no agreement (1 Timothy 2:1-3). Do we believe God? Then, let's walk God's talk in prayer!

He directs by His Holy Spirit to initiate reconciliation and, as much as it depends on us, to live in peace (Matthew 5:23-24; Romans 12:18). Walk God's talk in peace!

His command to think on that which is true, pure, honest, just, lovely, of virtue and a good report rings loud and clear (Philippians 4:8). Walk God's talk in thought!

God speaks a word of correction to us, "Be ye holy; for I am holy" (1 Peter 1:16). God's talk dictates our walk, when we, like Father Abraham, believe.

CONCLUSION

This righteousness of Abraham and those of us who believe God, His Word, and His promises are given a believing faith, not a wishing faith. Neither Abraham nor we have bragging rights. Just as it was with Abraham, so it is with us: we think of ourselves with sober judgment, by the measure of faith God has distributed (freely given) to each of us (Romans 12:3). It is the gift of God.

Father Abraham's faith, yours, and mine compel us to believe, move, WALK. We believe because of the One who said so. The One who cannot lie, who has all power to perform what He says, the One who has gone before us, the Greater One living His life through us, and walking alongside us all the way to His purposed finish line.

NOTES

_____

_____

_____

_____

_____

The Price of Salvation

By Rev. Jaimie Crumley

Lesson Theme	Unit Theme	Scripture
Justification through Faith	Faith and Salvation	Romans 5:1–11

INTRODUCTION

Maybe you have heard the phrase, "There is no such thing as a free lunch." By this, we mean that even those things we take for granted come at a price. Since humanity first sinned and became separated from God, God's primary goal has been reconciliation with us. God sent Jesus to be the sacrificial Lamb for the sins of the world. Although salvation is free to us, we must be ever mindful that salvation is not free. Let us live lives that are worthy of the incredible sacrifice Jesus made for us.

MESSAGE POINTS

Message Point 1: Justified (Romans 5:1–2)

Where do you turn when you are seeking approval and validation? In this fast-paced, social media age, we often feel pressure to earn the approval of people we hardly know. However, yearning for acceptance from others is not only a tendency of our present age. Members of the early church in Rome also sought to be accepted by their family members, neighbors, and associates. Paul wrote to members of the Roman church to assure them that through Christ Jesus, they were declared blameless. Although they were still sinners, they would share in the glory of God because of the deep and abiding love of Jesus Christ for them. Friends, these words of assurance apply to us as well. Although we are still sinners, God absolves and forgives us. We are already justified, approved, and validated by Jesus Christ, and we will share in the glory of God.

Message Point 2: Holy Boasting (vv. 3–5)

Throughout the Bible, we are urged to live with humility and not to be too proud. However, as followers of Jesus Christ, the one thing that we can boast about is the fact that we serve a God who has forgiven us, loves us, and invites us to share in God's glory. For that reason, even when we endure the struggles of this life, we can hold our heads high. Our struggles are part of the work of building our character. Take heart and do not give up. Allow the Holy Spirit to be your friend and advocate. Boast because God is with you and that the victory is already won in Jesus' name.

Message Point 3: Saved by His Life (vv. 6–11)

Salvation comes at a price. Before Jesus came to earth and showed us how to live sacrificially, atonement could only be achieved through the blood of animals. Humans lived in an adversarial relationship with our Creator. Jesus was sent to earth to show us another way to live. Although we did nothing to earn Jesus' sacrifice for us, He showed us that God called us to lay down our lives, even for our enemies. As followers of Christ, we are called to learn from the witness of Jesus Christ in the world. Jesus taught us to forgive, love, heal, and sacrifice for others. Let us be moved to live in ways that are worthy of the incredible sacrifice He made for us.

93

A theme that many theologians, authors, activists, and authors have grappled within their work is the question of how we are called to relate to each other as human beings. What are our responsibilities to each other, and how will we know whether we have lived up to those responsibilities? These are complex questions, and Romans 5:1–11 offers a potential response. What we owe to each other is to live sacrificially for others in the way that Jesus lived sacrificially for us. Before God sent Jesus to save us, we had done nothing to earn everlasting love. However, throughout His time on earth, Jesus offered forgiveness of sins, Jesus gave sight to the blind, Jesus raised the dead, Jesus gave justice to widows and orphans, Jesus provided living water. With Jesus' help, we can learn to love even those who persecute us and to make sacrifices for those who are yearning for God's grace.

CONCLUSION

You are justified by faith and have received full access to the depth of God's love for you. You can be proud of the incredible grace you have received. Go out and tell everyone you know that God's grace is real and that it is available to each one of us. You will still go through hardships in this life, but as you endure them, tell your problems about the incredible God you serve. God's grace will get you through even the most difficult challenges of this life. Do not take your salvation for granted. Yes, we are justified, but our justification was made possible through the blood of our crucified Savior. Learn from the life of the One who made the ultimate sacrifice for each of us. Live in ways that draw others close to the overwhelming, life-changing grace of God.

NOTES

_____

_____

_____

_____

_____

_____

_____

_____

_____

_____

_____

Effective Witnessing

By Dr. Timothy K. Beougher

Lesson Theme	Unit Theme	Scripture
Salvation for All Who Believe	Faith and Salvation	Romans 10:5–17

INTRODUCTION

Do you have a friend or loved one that you want to share the Gospel with? Maybe it's a co-worker or classmate who needs Jesus, but you just don't know how to be effective? In our passage today, Paul models five principles of an effective witness. Allow God's Word to encourage and challenge you this morning as you seek to reach out to others with God's love.

MESSAGE POINTS

Message Point 1: Comprehend People's Lost Condition (Romans 10:5–7)

People who live and die without knowing Christ are lost. They are lost now, and they will be lost for all of eternity; that's the straightforward message of our Scripture. Paul refers to the Jewish people he discussed in 9:32, whom he notes pursued righteousness as if it were to be attained by works. Israel's problem was self-righteousness. They wanted to make up their own rules instead of following God's rules. They did not want to accept God's righteousness as a gift of grace; they wanted to earn it by their own human efforts. Thus, they placed themselves under a standard by which they would ultimately be judged and found sadly lacking (v. 5). Christ gives His righteousness to all who believe (v. 4). Jesus lived a perfect life so we don't have to! That's why Paul notes (vv. 6–7) that we don't have to somehow get to heaven to find Christ, or to go into the realm of the dead. Salvation is found in simple faith and trust in Jesus Christ. Anyone depending on his or her efforts instead of trusting in God's righteousness is lost.

Message Point 2: Understand the Gospel (vv. 8–13)

The confession "Jesus is Lord" is at the heart of the response to the Gospel because it combines the twin responses of repentance and faith. Acknowledging Jesus as Lord indicates our acceptance that He is truly God; we place our faith in Him. It also means we remove ourselves from the throne of our life to live for ourselves and enthrone Christ as Lord; we repent of our sin. The confession with the mouth is a natural response to believing in the heart. Verse 12 reminds us that the Gospel is universal. Regardless of your background, Jesus Christ saves all who come to Him in genuine repentance and faith. Verse 13 summarizes the Gospel, which is by grace through faith.

Message Point 3: Share the Gospel (vv. 14–17)

Paul begins a series of rhetorical questions in verse 14. These questions conclude that the Lord does His work through His people. We must share the Gospel! The greatest thing we can do is to be messengers of the Good News. It's a message with a life-changing, worldwide impact, and we are the messengers!

Many children's books play with the idea of cause and effect. It's an important topic that takes children many years to learn. Books like "If You Give a Mouse a Cookie" or the "Choose Your Own Adventure" books go forward presenting a cause then showing the effect. Other books, like "The End" by David LaRochelle or "The Day Jimmy's Boa Ate the Wash" by Trinka Hakes Noble, build their stories going backward. "The Day Jimmy's Boa Ate the Wash" begins with a girl telling her mom about her class field trip to the farm: It was ok until the cow started crying. Why was a cow crying? Because a haystack fell on it. Why did the haystack fall? A farmer pushed it over with his tractor. Why would the farmer do that? He was distracted by the pigs jumping on our school bus and eating our lunches. And so on.

Paul is also interested in making sure his audience understood the cause and effect of Christianity. How can you be saved? You have to call on Jesus. How do you call on Jesus? You have to believe. How do you believe? You have to hear. How do you hear? Someone has to tell you. Where does that person come from? They have to be sent.

We have the power to send people out. We have the power and the knowledge to preach the Gospel. We can be the cause for spreading the Gospel, and praise God for its most glorious effect!

CONCLUSION

You may say, "I'm not sure I know enough. I'm not sure I would do a very good job in this type of ministry." The bottom line is to begin where you are. If you wait until you have mastered every approach, anticipated every question, read every book, etc., you will never do anything for the lost! You may legitimately feel like there is so much more you could know about sharing your faith. But don't let that stop you from reaching out to others around you right now!

NOTES

_____

_____

_____

_____

_____

_____

_____

_____

_____

_____

Faith Factors

By Pastor Rosalyn Bates

Lesson Theme	**Unit Theme**	**Scripture**
Meaning of Faith	Faith Gives Us Hope	Hebrews 11:1–8, 13–16

INTRODUCTION

Many people have been awestruck after they visited the Pro Football Hall of Fame, where football heroes are named and celebrated for their athletic achievements. The book of Hebrews was written to Hebrew Christians and maybe second-generation Christians in the first century, a time when they were facing social and physical persecution from other Jews and Romans. These Hebrew Christians lacked a temple or a central meeting place. They did not have any priests or sacrifices to offer. There was no order of worship at their services. These people were in transition, emotionally tense, economically deprived, and homeless. They were out of their element, disturbed, and unstable. What they needed was to be convinced that they should keep their faith in Christ instead of going back to their old practices. Chapter 11 of the book of Hebrews, which you could also call "the Pro Faith Hall of Fame," names the heroes and heroines of the faith in the history of Israel. This chapter commends them for their tenacious trust in God so that Hebrew Christians who were struggling to maintain their faith in Christ might be encouraged.

MESSAGE POINTS

Message Point 1: Faith Connects the Invisible with the Visible (Hebrews 11:1–3)

Faith is expressed by our words, and words create our world. At God's command, His word, the whole universe was created. In the beginning, God spoke, "Let there be" and it happened. He declared—whether it was light, the heavens and earth, or creatures—and it came into being from nothing. God created simply by speaking. Before God uttered any words, the earth had qualities of emptiness, shapelessness, and lack of structure. God's words carry life and power. Similarly, life and death are in the power of what we speak. Our faith in God can speak volumes. Although they are invisible themselves, the words that we speak create visible things. Even though our situation may appear empty, void and lifeless, words of faith will not only sustain hope in our hearts; they will also call something of value into existence. Words of faith as inspired by God insert God's divine order into areas that are disorganized and make productive what would otherwise be fruitless.

Message Point 2: Faith Links the Present with the Future (vv. 4–8)

Faith links what is going on now with what is going to happen. It is not wishful thinking; faith is a confident expectation based on God's faithfulness. Having faith means that one is living eagerly concerning God's promise. This attitude of wonder and anticipation pleases God. It makes God smile. This is a direct challenge to people who worry and stay guarded with low expectations. Abraham, the father of faith, listens to God's call to leave his homeland without knowing his next destination. He packs his bags and moves. He expects God to lead and show him the next place, the land of his inheritance. He could have maintained his comfort and security, unchallenged in his homeland, but instead, Abraham sacrificially organizes his life around getting what God said He would give to him. Abraham was future-minded and did not allow uncertainty to keep him neutral. He allowed his faith in God to take him in the direction of promise. Do you ever ask God, "What's next?" and wonder where your faith in God is taking you?

Message Point 3: Faith Applies Beyond One's Years (vv. 13–16)
Faith in God impacts the current generation and the generations that follow. The heroes and heroines faithfully believed in God's promise for them in their times, even if the promise was not fulfilled in their times. The Scripture tells us that they saw the promise from a distance, knowing that God's promise was not limited to the years that they lived. They understood that what God does extends far beyond their lifespan and it involved their legacy. The heroes and heroines understood that God is their God and also the God of their lineage. Frequently, God is identified as "the God of Abraham, and of Isaac, and of Jacob" (Exodus 3:16; Acts 3:13). As modern-day believers in Christ, our faith is strengthened when we reflect on the journeys of those who trusted God in times past. God's promise, coupled with their long-range vision, made room for the generations ahead to be blessed. We are similarly challenged to embrace God's promises for our own generation while posturing the next generations to journey faithfully.

THAT'LL PREACH

Faith is a vision, but not merely sight because faith challenges us to see more than what appears to our natural eyes. Faith pushes us to pursue with imagination what God has promised. First Corinthians 2:9 tells us, "Eye hath not seen, nor ear heard, neither have entered into the heart of man, the things which God hath prepared for them that love him." Verse 10 follows by telling us that God reveals to us the things He has prepared for us by His Spirit. The people of faith listed in Hebrews 11 obeyed practically, but they were not limited by their own realities because they received God's introduction to what they never naturally thought was possible. Ask the Lord to be your vision so that you may walk by faith and beyond the reality that you see with your natural eyes.

CONCLUSION

Faith is the essential factor of our hope in Jesus Christ. It connects the human with the divine, the visible with the invisible, and the present with the future. Faith will take us on a journey with God, who will never leave us or forsake us. As we go, we grow in our understanding of faith's value to God, to us, and to generations to come.

NOTES

_____

_____

_____

_____

_____

_____

_____

_____

Explaining Hard Verses

By Beth Potterveld

Lesson Theme	**Unit Theme**	**Scripture**
A Persevering Faith	Faith Gives Us Hope	Hebrews 10:23–36

INTRODUCTION

There are some hard verses in Scripture. Hebrews 10:26 is one of them: "For if we sin willfully after that we have received the knowledge of the truth, there remaineth no more sacrifice for sins." Does that mean if I knowingly sin after I become a Christian, no sacrifice can save me anymore? Does that mean after I prayed the Sinner's Prayer when I was 8 years old, I wasn't supposed to sin anymore? I know I have. Did the prayer not work? Am I not truly saved? The verse springs up so many questions and doubts. What do we do with this kind of verse? How do we deal with hard verses?

When one part of Scripture is unclear, we look to a clearer part of Scripture to explain the unclear parts. Let's see what other verses say about Hebrews 10:26.

MESSAGE POINTS

Message Point 1: The Sinner (Hebrews 10:26)

It's not about Christians who sin. There are some Christians who believe you don't actually sin after being saved, partially because of this verse. But that's not what the writer of Hebrews is talking about. We know that true believers still sin. Look at Peter, who needed a stern talking to from Paul about eating with Gentiles (Galatians 2:11). Look at Mark, who deserted Paul on the missionary trail, but then was a faithful companion on later trips (Acts 15:37–39; 2 Timothy 4:11). Look at your own life. Christians will still sin and still be forgiven. The blood has the power to cleanse ANY sin if we choose it.

Message Point 2: The Apostate (vv. 27-31)

"If we choose it" being the operative clause. Some see the cross, and still, ask God to do more. Some see Christ's new covenant and don't understand what it would mean for them if they would only trust God. "Sure Jesus did that, but why doesn't He also… [fill in the blank]?" If THEY had ultimate power and authority, they surely would make sure nobody ever suffered. Oh, child. If Jesus' death and resurrection don't convince you that God has a plan and has everything under control, nothing will. If you think Jesus' blood is common, you will not respect anything. If you can see the suffering Jesus endured (just so you could join Him in eternity) and still not trust that He knows how it feels to be human, you will never understand empathy. If your knowledge of Christ's glorious sacrifice and promise of eternal redemption isn't enough to convince you to follow God's law, nothing will. There's no better sacrifice that God can entice you with.

Message Point 3: The Sanctified (vv. 23-25, 32-36)

If you forget what a great deal we have in Christ, you will deliberately sin and there's no helping you. If you remember what a great deal we have in Christ, you will hold on to hope, encourage others, meet together, and suffer persecution. Because you have hope, trust, and faith in God's promise: you know Christ will return to reign. We have hope in our ability to approach God because Christ is our high priest. We are promised Christ will return, bringing us salvation and blessing, a heavenly city and citizenship within it.

THAT'LL PREACH

On July 8, 1741, Jonathan Edwards first preached what has become his most famous sermon: "Sinners in the Hands of an Angry God." In it, he explains a small phrase in Deuteronomy 32:35 about sinners falling, exploring how and why God exacts judgment on those who have chosen not to follow Him. Edwards paints a fiery picture of a sinner dangerously close to falling down into the judgment they have earned as the natural outcome of their deeds. The only thing suspending them from this fatal fall is the barest string of God's "arbitrary mercy." God's hand of mercy alone holds the sinners, and God doesn't even like them. He is angry with the sinner, looking at him as "some loathsome insect." They are sinners in the hand of an angry God. And as Hebrews 10:31 says, "It is a fearful thing to fall into the hands of the living God." This is another hard verse. But I invite you to read—or better, listen—to Edward's sermon as he brings up verse after verse of Scripture to help his congregation understand the urgent call to salvation. With clearer, easier verses, he helps them understand the hard verses about God.

CONCLUSION

The more we read Scripture, the more we understand the vast God we serve. While we will never completely grasp the fullness of our infinite God, He has given us His Word, so we can plum its depths to learn about our God from its pages. We will learn He is a holy God, a powerful God, a just God, a merciful God, a beautiful God. We can't fully understand Him this side of glory, but we have His Word, so let's try anyway! Let's build each other up. Let's meet together. Let's hold fast to the promises of our great God.

NOTES

_____

_____

_____

_____

_____

_____

_____

_____

Do You Have The Right Credentials?

By Ramon Mayo

Lesson Theme	**Unit Theme**	**Scripture**
A Conquering Faith	Faith Gives Us Hope	1 John 4:2–3, 13–17; 5:4-5

INTRODUCTION

Your passport lets people know you are a citizen of a certain country. It's the credentials that allow you access to everything you are entitled to as a citizen. When you have a driver's license, you are given the right to drive. When you have a user name and password to a certain website or app, you have credentials that give you access to the benefits or functionality of that technology. So what are our credentials for the life God wants us to experience? Many times you experience roadblocks and obstacles in your spiritual life because you don't have the right credentials.

1 John is all about how to know if you have the right credentials for the spiritual life. There were some folks in John's day called the Gnostics who were saying the right spiritual credentials were knowledge but 1 John says knowledge is not the credentials God requires. Today we're going to look at 1 John 4:2–3 and 13–17 to take a look at those credentials. And so my question to you today is: Do you have the right credentials?

MESSAGE POINTS

Message Point 1: You need to confess and know who Jesus is
Back in John's day, folks were saying Jesus didn't come as God in the flesh. They couldn't comprehend God having a body. This is the beauty and the mystery of the incarnation. Not only did He have a body but He also experienced the same things we did. Jesus was God and man.

The first Christian credential you need to check is whether you confess and know who Jesus is. So many people nowadays think Jesus is just a good moral teacher or a prophet of justice. The truth is He was those things but He is so much more: He is the Son of God who came in the flesh. Anything other than this is an antichrist belief and the wrong credentials.

Message Point 2: You need to receive the Holy Spirit
The next credential you need is the Holy Spirit. This is where we find proof of our relationship with God. It's the witness of the Spirit that is the evidence of our belonging to him. John adds that he and the other apostles saw Him with their eyes, but that is not a privilege we in the 21st century have.

We only can know Him through the Spirit and His "living in us." How do we know He lives in us? When we declare Jesus is the Son of God sent to be the Savior of the World! Nobody can say this without the help of the Holy Spirit. This is our proof and our credential of belonging to the same family as the Father and the Son.

Message Point 3: You need to live a life of love

And then there's the last credential: a life of love. You can't say Jesus is the Son of God and have the Holy Spirit living within you and live a loveless life. Without love it is meaningless. It's the last layer of credentials, and it's very important.

You can have all of your doctrines right. You can go to church. You can pay your tithes. But if you are mean as a Rottweiler, then you can't say you are a part of God's family. When you don't actively seek to pursue the best interest of the people around you, then you are missing the last credential. Those who confess Jesus is the Son of God and have the Holy Spirit must also have the love of Jesus and the Holy Spirit or else their profession is meaningless. Love is the last credential.

THAT'LL PREACH

Once while on a mission trip to Ethiopia our plane had to make an unexpected stop in Khartoum, Sudan for a day due to weather. Not only was this a setback to our scheduled time of arrival, but when we got off the plane, the airport officials directed us to leave our passports with the airport security. So we were without our passports for a whole day. It was a weird and scary experience because if anything happened, we could not be identified as American citizens. The same thing goes for our spiritual life. It's why our spiritual credentials are so important. Without them, we live in a state of fear and anxiety.

CONCLUSION

The right credentials get you access to different things. The right spiritual credentials let you know where you stand with God. Having the right spiritual credentials doesn't make you a part of an exclusive holy club but puts you on an inclusive holy mission to love others. When you have the right credentials, you have access to all the resources God has to bless your community and the world. When you have the right credentials, you enter into the same mission as the Father, Son, and Holy Spirit to tackle the oppression, injustice, and evil we see in the world. We have their power and wisdom, so we're not just going it alone. It's good to have the right credentials.

NOTES

_____

_____

_____

_____

_____

_____

_____

_____

Tackling Life with Confidence

By Robert Morgan

Lesson Theme	Unit Theme	Scripture
Hope Eternal	Faith Gives Us Hope	2 Corinthians 4:16–5:10

INTRODUCTION

If you go down to your favorite bookstore, you could come home with a shopping bag containing these books: "Confidence: How Winning Streaks and Losing Streaks Begin and End", "How to Develop Self-Confidence and Influence People", "Ultimate Secrets of Total Self-Confidence", "How to Have Confidence and Power in Dealing with People", "The Confident Woman", "Raising Confident Boys", "Raising Confident Girls", "Ten Days to More Confident Public Speaking", "A Guide to Confident Living", "The Confident Coach's Guide to Teaching Soccer", "How to Be Your Own Therapist: A Step-by-Step Guide to Building a Confident Life", and "Bombproof Your Horse: Teach Your Horse to Be Confident, Obedient, and Safe, No Matter What You Encounter". All of us want to tackle life with confidence—we want that for ourselves and our children, our students, and even for our horses. Well, if you want to know the ultimate secrets to total self-confidence, then read 2 Corinthians. Paul uses the words "confident" and "confidence" twelve times here. He's a man who has been rejected, ridiculed, beaten, battered, criticized, and vilified. But his opponents were totally stymied when it came to shaking his confidence. He said, "I know, I am confident, I am always confident."

MESSAGE POINTS

Message Point 1: Confident People Think a Great Deal About Heaven (2 Corinthians 4:16–5:4)

Verse 1 is really the direct continuation of the previous paragraph, which, in our Bibles, is at the end of chapter 4. In life, we have momentary troubles, like little weights on one side of the scale. But we are heirs of life in Christ with all that comes with that—the new heavens, the new earth, the New Jerusalem, the new order of things—and when that's on the other side of the scale, there's no comparison. So we fix our eyes on what is unseen. Whenever we're tempted to lose heart, we think about heaven. Our bodies are merely tents that will collapse at some point, but we have an eternal house in the heavens, not made by human hands. Paul tells us our bodies are like tents, temporary dwellings. At some point, we loosen the cords, pull up the stakes, collapse the tent, and pack it away. We long for our heavenly dwelling; and when we think about heaven, it gives us confidence in the future.

Message Point 2: Confident People Draw on Inner Resources (v. 5)

God, Himself is preparing us for the experience of putting on immortality and eternal life. As a down payment guaranteeing what is to come, He has given us the inner resources of the Holy Spirit. That power is always within every Christian. With that power, Jesus promised we could do even greater things than He did. With that power, we can know exactly what to say when asked to defend our Christianity. With that power, we can move mountains.

Message Point 3: Confident People Want to Please Christ (vv. 6–10)

The third mark of confident people is a desire to please Christ. When our goal in life is to please the Lord, it inspires confidence because we know we're on the right road. And the great thing about pleasing Him is that we can do it on both sides of the grave. So we make it our goal to please Him, whether we are at home in the body or away from it.

THAT'LL PREACH

Some time ago, I was driving to a speaking engagement and I became disoriented on the road and wondered if I was taking the right route. I didn't have very much time to spare, and I felt a sense of panic. I tried to call someone on my cell phone, but couldn't get anyone. I tried to read my directions as I drove, but couldn't make heads or tails of them. Frustration rose up inside me until suddenly I saw a familiar landmark. My confidence returned because I knew I was on the right road after all.

CONCLUSION

Many of us struggle with self-doubt, shyness, and a sense of inferiority. But the Bible says: "If God be for us, who can be against us?" (from Romans 8:31). In the closing moments of this message, I want to encourage each of you to preach a little sermon to yourself. I can't be around you 24 hours a day to preach to you all the time, and many of my sermons aren't what you need anyway. I want to deputize you and show you how to preach to the hardest congregation of all—yourself. Confident people preach to themselves from the truth of God's Word. They remind themselves of His promises.

So here's your sermon: I am full of confidence today because:
• God the Father has a house for me in the heavens, not built by human hands.
• God the Spirit lives within me as a divine deposit.

NOTES

_____

_____

_____

_____

_____

_____

_____

_____

_____

_____

_____